Georg Bühler, James Burgess

On the Indian Sect of the Jainas

Georg Bühler, James Burgess

On the Indian Sect of the Jainas

ISBN/EAN: 9783337537692

Printed in Europe, USA, Canada, Australia, Japan

Cover: Foto ©Andreas Hilbeck / pixelio.de

More available books at **www.hansebooks.com**

ON THE INDIAN SECT OF THE JAINAS

BY
JOHANN GEORG BÜHLER C.I.E., LLD., PH.D.
Member of the Imperial Academy of Sciences, Vienna.

TRANSLATED FROM THE GERMAN.

EDITED
with an
OUTLINE of JAINA MYTHOLOGY

BY
JAS. BURGESS, C.I.E., LL.D., F.R.S.E.

1903.

CONTENTS.

Non-Unicode Edition
Transliterated to Latin-1 Extended characters using the recommendations of the University of Massachusett's "Indian Text Survey" project, as explained at http://www.umass.edu/wsp/indica/recommended/sanskrit.html.

Unicode Edition
Uses unicode combining characters to reproduce the transliteration scheme of the original 1903 document. Unfortunately support for these characters is not yet perfect, so they will not display correctly on older browsers and operating systems.

Note to the HTML edition: The Sanskrit in this document has been transliterated from the 1906 original according to the recommendations of the University of Massachusett's "Indian Text Survey" project, as explained at http://www.umass.edu/wsp/indica/recommended/sanskrit.html.

ON THE INDIAN SECT OF THE JAINAS

BY
JOHANN GEORG BÜHLER C.I.E., LLD., PH.D.
Member of the Imperial Academy of Sciences, Vienna.

TRANSLATED FROM THE GERMAN.

EDITED
with an
OUTLINE of JAINA MYTHOLOGY

BY
JAS. BURGESS, C.I.E., LL.D., F.R.S.E.

1903.

CONTENTS.

Preface

THE INDIAN SECT OF THE JAINAS,
by Dr. J. G. BÜHLER.

Appendix:
Epigraphic testimony to the continuity of the Jaina tradition
[Fig. 1] [Fig. 2] [Fig. 3] [Fig. 4] [Fig. 5] [Fig. 6] [Fig. 7]

Footnotes

SKETCH OF JAINA MYTHOLOGY,
by J. BURGESS.

The Gachhas of the Jainas

Footnotes

PREFACE.

The late Dr. Georg Bühler's essay *Ueber die Indische Secte der Jaina*, read at the anniversary meeting of the Imperial Academy of Sciences of Vienna on the 26th May 1887, has been for some time out of print in the separate form. Its value as a succinct account of the Śrâvaka sect, by a scholar conversant with them and their religious literature is well known to European scholars; but to nearly all educated natives of India works published in German and other continental languages are practically sealed books, and thus the fresh information which they are well able to contribute is not elicited. It is hoped that the translation of this small work may meet with their acceptance and that of Europeans in India and elsewhere to whom the original is either unknown or who do not find a foreign language so easy to read as their own.

The translation has been prepared under my supervision, and with a few short footnotes. Professor Bühler's long note on the authenticity of the Jaina tradition I have transferred to an appendix (p. 48) incorporating with it a summary of what he subsequently expanded in proof of his thesis.

To Colebrooke's account of the Tirtham[postvocalic] karas reverenced by the Jainas, but little has been added since its publication in the ninth volume of the *Asiatic Researches*; and as these are the centre of their worship, always represented in their temples, and surrounded by attendant figures,--I have ventured to add a somewhat fuller account of them and a summary of the general mythology of the sect, which may be useful to the archaeologist and the student of their iconography.

Edinburgh, April 1903. **J. BURGESS.**

THE INDIAN SECT OF THE JAINAS.

The *Jaina* sect is a religious society of modern India, at variance to Brahmanism, and possesses undoubted claims on the interest of all friends of Indian history. This claim is based partly on the peculiarities of their doctrines and customs, which present several resemblances to those of Buddhism, but, above all, on the fact that it was founded in the same period as the latter.

Larger and smaller communities of *Jainas* or *Arhata*,--that is followers of the prophet, who is generally called simply the *Jina*--'the conqueror of the world',--or the *Arhat*--'the holy one',--are to be found in almost every important Indian town, particularly among the merchant class. In some provinces of the West and North-west, in Gujarât, Râjputâna, and the Panjâb, as also in the Dravidian districts in the south,--especially in Kanara,--they are numerous; and, owing to the influence of their wealth, they take a prominent place. They do not, however, present a compact mass, but are divided into two rival branches--the *Digambara* and *Śvetâmbara*[1] --each of which is split up into several subdivisions. The Digambara, that is, "those whose robe is the atmosphere," owe their name to the circumstance that they regard absolute nudity as the indispensable sign of holiness, [2] --though the advance of civilization has compelled them to depart from the practice of their theory. The Śvetâmbara, that is, "they who are clothed in white"--do not claim this doctrine, but hold it as possible that the holy ones, who clothe themselves, may also attain the highest goal. They allow, however, that the founder of the Jaina religion and his first disciples disdained to wear clothes. They are divided, not only by this quarrel, but also by differences about dogmas and by a different literature. The separation must therefore be of old standing. Tradition, too, upholds this--though the dates given do not coincide. From inscriptions it is certain that the split occurred before the first century of our era. [3] Their opposing opinions are manifested in the fact that they do not allow each other the right of intermarriage or of eating at the same table,--the two chief marks of social equality. In spite of the age of the schism, and the enmity that divides the two branches, they are at one as regards the arrangement of their communities, doctrine, discipline, and cult,--at least in the more important points; and, thus, one can always speak of the Jaina religion as a whole.

The characteristic feature of this religion is its claim to universality, which it holds in common with Buddhism, and in opposition to Brahmanism. It also declares its object to be to lead all men to salvation, and to open its arms--not only to the noble Aryan, but also to the low-born Śûdra and even to the alien, deeply despised in India, the Mlechcha. [4] As their doctrine, like Buddha's, is originally a philosophical ethical system intended for ascetics, the disciples, like the Buddhists, are, divided into ecclesiastics and laity. At the head stands an order of ascetics, originally Nirgrantha "they, who are freed from all bands," now usually called Yatis--"Ascetics", or Sâdhus--"Holy", which, among the Śvetâmbara also admits women, [5] and under them the general community of the Upâsaka "the Worshippers", or the Śrâvaka, "the hearers".

The ascetics alone are able to penetrate into the truths which Jina teaches, to follow his rules and to attain to the highest reward which he promises. The laity, however, who do not dedicate themselves to the search after truth, and cannot renounce the life of the world, still find a refuge in Jainism. It is allowed to them as hearers to share its principles, and to undertake duties, which are a faint copy of the demands made on the ascetics. Their reward is naturally less. He who remains in the world cannot reach the highest goal, but he can still tread the way which leads to it. Like all religions of the Hindûs founded on philosophical speculation, Jainism sees this highest goal in *Nirvâna* or *Moksha*, the setting free of the individual from the *Sam[postvocalic] sâra*,--the revolution of birth and death. The means of reaching it are to it, as to Buddhism, the three Jewels--the right Faith, the right Knowledge, and the right Walk. By the right Faith it understands the full surrender of himself to the teacher, the Jina, the firm conviction that he alone has found the way of salvation, and only with him is protection and refuge to be found. Ask who Jina is, and the Jaina will give exactly the same answer as the Buddhist with respect to

Buddha. He is originally an erring man, bound with the bonds of the world, who,--not by the help of a teacher, nor by the revelation of the Vedas--which, he declares, are corrupt--but by his own power, has attained to omniscience and freedom, and out of pity for suffering mankind preaches and declares the way of salvation, which he has found. Because he has conquered the world and the enemies in the human heart, he is called Jina "the Victor", Mahâvîra, "the great hero"; because he possesses the highest knowledge, he is called Sarvajña or Kevalin, the "omniscient", Buddha, the "enlightened"; because he has freed himself from the world he receives the names of Mukta "the delivered one", Siddha and Tathâgata, "the perfected", Arhat "the holy one"; and as the proclaimer of the doctrine, he is the Tîrthakara "the finder of the ford", through the ocean of the *Sam[postvocalic] sâra*. In these epithets, applied to the founder of their doctrine, the Jainas agree almost entirely with the Buddhists, as the likeness of his character to that of Buddha would lead us to expect. They prefer, however, to use the names Jina and Arhat, while the Buddhists prefer to speak of Buddha as Tathâgata or Sugata. The title Tîrthakara is peculiar to the Jainas. Among the Buddhists it is a designation for false teachers. [6]

The Jaina says further, however, that there was more than one Jina. Four and twenty have, at long intervals, appeared and have again and again restored to their original purity the doctrines darkened by evil influences. They all spring from noble, warlike tribes. Only in such, not among the low Brâhma*n*s, can a Jina see the light of the world. The first Jina R ıshabha,--more than 100 billion oceans of years ago,--periods of unimaginable length, [7] --was born as the son of a king of Ayodhyâ and lived eight million four hundred thousand years. The intervals between his successors and the durations of their lives became shorter and shorter. Between the twenty third, Pârśva and the twenty fourth Vardhamâna, were only 250 years, and the age of the latter is given as only seventy-two years. He appeared, according to some, in the last half of the sixth century, according to others in the first half of the fifth century B.C. He is of course the true, historical prophet of the Jainas and it is in his doctrine, that the Jainas should believe. The dating back of the origin of the Jaina religion again, agrees with the pretensions of the Buddhists, who recognise twenty-five Buddhas who taught the same system one after the other. Even with Brahmanism, it seems to be in some distant manner connected, for the latter teaches in its cosmogony, the successive appearance of Demiurges, and wise men--the fourteen Manus, who, at various periods helped to complete the work of creation and proclaimed the Brahmanical law. These Brahmanical ideas may possibly have given rise to the doctrines of the twenty-five Buddhas and twenty-four Jinas, [8] which, certainly, are later additions in both systems.

The undoubted and absolutely correct comprehension of the nine truths which the Jina gives expression to, or of the philosophical system which the Jina taught, represents the second Jewel--the true Knowledge. Its principal features are shortly as follows. [9]

The world (by which we are to understand, not only the visible, but also imaginary continents depicted with the most extravagant fancy, heavens and hells of the Brahmanical Cosmology, extended by new discoveries) is uncreated. It exists, without ruler, only by the power of its elements, and is everlasting. The elements of the world are six substances--souls, *Dharma* or moral merit, *Adharma* or sin, space, time, particles of matter. From the union of the latter spring four elements--earth, fire, water, wind--and further, bodies and all other appearances of the world of sense and of the supernatural worlds. The forms of the appearances are mostly unchangeable. Only the bodies of men and their age increase or decrease in consequence of the greater or less influence of sin or merit, during immeasurably long periods,--the *Avasarpin i* and the *Utsarpin i*. Souls are, each by itself, independent, real existences whose foundation is pure intelligence, and who possess an impulse to action. In the world they are always chained to bodies. The reason of this confinement is that they give themselves up to the stress of activity, to passions, to influences of the senses and objects of the mind, or attach themselves to a false belief. The deeds which they perform in the bodies are *Karman*, merit and sin. This drives them--when one body has passed away, according to the conditions of its existence--into another, whose quality depends on the character of the *Karman*, and will be determined especially by the last thoughts springing from it before death. Virtue leads to the heavens of the gods or to birth among men in pure and noble races. Sin consigns the souls to the lower regions, in the bodies of animals, in plants, even into masses of lifeless matter. For--according to the Jaina doctrine--souls exist not only in organic structures, but also in apparently dead masses, in stones, in lumps of earth, in drops of water, in fire and in wind. Through union with bodies the nature of the soul is affected. In the mass of matter the light of its intelligence is completely concealed; it loses consciousness, is immovable, and large or small, according to the dimensions of its abode. In organic structures it is always conscious; it depends however, on the nature of the same, whether it is movable or immovable and possessed of five, four, three, two, or one organ of sense.

The bondage of souls, if they inhabit a human body, can be abolished by the suppression of the causes which lead to their confinement and by the destruction of the *Karman*. The suppression of the causes is accomplished by overcoming the inclination to be active and the passions, by the control of the senses, and by steadfastly holding to the right faith. In this way will be hindered the addition of new *Karman*, new merit or new guilt. The destruction of *Karman* remaining from previous existences can be brought about either spontaneously by the exhaustion of the supply or by asceticism. In the latter case the final state is the attainment to a knowledge which penetrates the universe, to *Kevala, Jñâna* and *Nirvân a* or *Moksha*: full deliverance from all bonds. These goals may be reached even while the soul is still in its body. If however the body is destroyed then the soul wanders into the "No-World" *(alôka)* as the Jain says, i.e. into the heaven of Jina 'the delivered', lying outside the world. [10] There it continues eternally in its pure intellectual nature. Its condition is that of perfect rest which nothing disturbs. These fundamental ideas are carried out in the particulars with a subtilness and fantasy unexampled, even in subtile and fantastic India, in a scholarly style, and defended by the *syâdvâda*--the doctrine of "It may be so",--a mode of reasoning which makes it possible to assert and deny the existence of one and the same thing. If this be compared with the other Indian systems, it stands nearer the Brâhma*n* than the Buddhist, with which it has the acceptance in common of only four, not five elements. Jainism touches all the Brâhma*n* religions and Buddhism in its cosmology and ideas of periods, and it agrees entirely with regard to the doctrines of *Karman*, of the bondage, and the deliverance of souls. Atheism, the view that the world was not created, is common to it with Buddhism and the Sâm[postvocalic] khya philosophy. Its psychology approaches that of the latter in that both believe in the existence of innumerable independent souls. But the doctrine of the activity of souls and their distribution into masses of matter is in accordance with the Vedânta, according to which the principle of the soul penetrates every thing existing. In the further development of the soul doctrine, the conceptions 'individual soul' and 'living being' to which the Jaina and the Brâhma*n* give the same name,--*jîva*, seem to become confounded. The Jaina idea of space and time as real substances is also found in the Vaiśeshika system. In placing *Dharma* and *Adharma* among substances Jainism stands alone.

The third jewel, the right Walk which the Jaina ethics contains, has its kernel in the five great oaths which the Jaina ascetic takes on his entrance into the order. He promises, just as the Brâhma*n* penitent, and almost in the same words, not to hurt, not to speak untruth, to appropriate nothing to himself without permission, to preserve chastity, and to practice self-sacrifice. The contents of these simple rules become most extraordinarily extended on the part of the Jainas by the insertion of five clauses, in each of which are three separate active instruments of sin, in special relation to thoughts, words, and deeds. Thus, concerning the oath not to hurt, on which the Jaina lays the greatest emphasis: it includes not only the intentional killing or hurting of living beings, plants, or the souls existing in dead matter, it requires also the utmost carefulness in the whole manner of life, in all movements, a watchfulness over all functions of the body by which anything living might be hurt. [11] It demands finally strict watch over the heart and tongue, and the avoidance of all thoughts and words which might lead to dispute and quarrel and thereby to harm. In like manner the rule of sacrifice means not only that the ascetic has no house or possessions, it teaches also that a complete unconcern toward agreeable and disagreeable impressions is necessary, as also the sacrifice of every attachment to anything living or dead. [12]

Beside the conscientious observance of these rules, Tapas--Asceticism, is most important for the right walk of those, who strive to attain *Nirvân a.* Asceticism is inward as well as outward. The former is concerned with self-discipline, the cleansing and purifying of the mind. It embraces repentance of sin, confession of the same to the teacher, and penance done for it, humility before teachers and all virtuous ones, and the service of the same, the study and teaching of the faith or holy writing, pious meditations on the misery of the world, the impurity of the body, etc. and lastly, the stripping off of every thing pertaining to the world. On the other hand, under the head of exterior Asceticism, the Jaina understands temperance, begging, giving up all savoury food, different kinds of self-mortification such as sitting in unnatural and wearying positions, hindering the action of the organs, especially by fasts, which, under certain circumstances may be continued to starvation. Voluntary death by the withdrawal of nourishment is, according to the strict doctrine of the Digambara, necessary for all ascetics, who have reached the highest step of knowledge. The Kevalin, they say, eats no longer. The milder Śvetâmbara do not demand this absolutely, but regard it, as a sure entrance to *Nirvân a*. In order, however, that this death may bear its fruits, the ascetic must keep closely to the directions for it, otherwise he merely lengthens the number of rebirths. [13]

From these general rules follow numerous special ones, regarding the life of the disciple of Jina. The duty of sacrifice forces him, on entrance into the order, to give up his possessions and wander homeless in strange lands, alms-vessel in hand, and, if no other duty interferes, never to stay longer than one night in the same place. The rule of wounding nothing means that he must carry three articles with him, a straining cloth, for his drinking water, a broom, and a veil before his mouth, in order to avoid killing insects. It also commands him to avoid all cleansing and washing, and to rest in the four months of the rainy season, in which animal and plant life displays itself most abundantly. In order to practice asceticism, it is the rule to make this time of rest a period of strictest fasts, most diligent study of the holy writings, and deepest meditation. This duty also necessitates the ascetic to pluck out in the most painful manner his hair which, according to oriental custom, he must do away with at his consecration--a peculiar custom of the Jainas, which is not found among other penitents of India.

Like the five great vows, most of the special directions for the discipline of the Jain ascetic are copies, and often exaggerated copies, of the Brâhmanic rules for penitents. The outward marks of the order closely resemble those of the Sannyâsin. The life of wandering during eight months and the rest during the rainy season agree exactly; and in many other points, for example in the use of confession, they agree with the Buddhists. They agree with Brâhma*n*s alone in ascetic self-torture, which Buddhism rejects; and specially characteristic is the fact that ancient Brâhmanism recommends starvation to its penitents as beneficial. [14]

The doctrine of the right way for the Jaina laity differs from that for the ascetics. In place of the five great vows appear mere echoes. He vows to avoid only serious injury to living beings, i.e. men and animals; only the grosser forms of untruth--direct lies; only the most flagrant forms of taking, what is not given, that is, theft and robbery. In place of the oath of chastity there is that of conjugal fidelity. In place of that of self-denial, the promise is not greedily to accumulate possessions and to be contented. To these copies are added seven other vows, the miscellaneous contents of which correspond to the special directions for the discipline of ascetics. Their object is, partly to bring the outward life of the laity into accordance with the Jaina teaching, especially with regard to the protection of living creatures from harm, and partly to point the heart to the highest goal. Some contain prohibitions against certain drinks, such as spirits; or meats, such as flesh, fresh butter, honey, which cannot be enjoyed without breaking the vow of preservation of animal life. Others limit the choice of businesses which the laity may enter; for example, agriculture is forbidden, as it involves the tearing up of the ground and the death of many animals, as Brâhmanism also holds. Others have to do with mercy and charitableness, with the preserving of inward peace, or with the necessity of neither clinging too much to life and its joys nor longing for death as the end of suffering. To the laity, however, voluntary starvation is also recommended as meritorious. These directions (as might be expected from the likeness of the circumstances) resemble in many points the Buddhist directions for the laity, and indeed are often identical with regard to the language used. Much is however specially in accordance with Brâhmanic doctrines. [15] In practical life Jainism makes of its laity earnest men who exhibit a stronger trait of resignation than other Indians and excel in an exceptional willingness to sacrifice anything for their religion. It makes them also fanatics for the protection of animal life. Wherever they gain influence, there is an end of bloody sacrifices and of slaughtering and killing the larger animals.

The union of the laity with the order of ascetics has, naturally, exercised a powerful reaction on the former and its development, as well as on its teaching, and is followed by similar results in Jainism and Buddhism. Then, as regards the changes in the teaching, it is no doubt to be ascribed to the influence of the laity that the atheistic Jaina system, as well as the Buddhist, has been endowed with a cult. The ascetic, in his striving for *Nirvân a*, endeavours to suppress the natural desire of man to worship higher powers. In the worldly hearer, who does not strive after this goal exclusively, this could not succeed. Since the doctrine gave no other support, the religious feeling of the laity clung to the founder of it: Jina, and with him his mythical predecessors, became gods. Monuments and temples ornamented with their statues were built, especially at those places, where the prophets, according to legends, had reached their goal. To this is added a kind of worship, consisting of offerings of flowers and incense to Jina, of adoration by songs of praise in celebration of their entrance into *Nirvân a*, of which the Jaina makes a great festival by solemn processions and pilgrimages to the places where it has been attained. [16] This influence of the laity has become, in course of time, of great importance to Indian art, and India is indebted to it for a number of its most beautiful architectural monuments, such as the splendid temples of Âbu, Girnâr and Śatruñjaya in Gujarât. It has also brought about a change in the mind of the ascetics. In many of their hymns in honour of Jina, they appeal to him with as much fervour as the Brâhma*n* to his gods; and there are often expressions in them, contrary, to the original teaching, ascribing to Jina a creative power. Indeed a Jaina description of the six principal systems goes so far as to number Jainism--as also Buddhism--among the theistic religions. [17]

But in other respects also the admission of the laity has produced decisive changes in the life of the clergy. In the education of worldly communities, the ascetic--whose rules of indifference toward all and every thing, make him a being concentrated entirely upon himself and his goal--is united again to humanity and its interests. The duty of educating the layman and watching over his life, must of necessity change the wandering penitents into settled monks--who dedicate themselves to the care of souls, missionary activity, and the acquisition of knowledge, and who only now and again fulfil the duty of changing their place of residence. The needs of the lay communities required the continual presence of teachers. Even should these desire to change from time to time, it was yet necessary to provide a shelter for them. Thus the Upâśraya or places of refuge, the Jaina monasteries came into existence, which exactly correspond to the Buddhist Sanghârâma. With the monasteries and the fixed residence in them appeared a fixed membership of the order, which, on account of the Jaina principle of unconditional obedience toward the teacher, proved to be much stricter than in Buddhism. On the development of the order and the leisure of monastic life, there followed further, the commencement of a literary and scientific activity. The oldest attempt, in this respect, limited itself to bringing their doctrine into fixed forms. Their results were, besides other lost works, the so-called *Am[postvocalic] ga*,--the members of the body of the law, which was perhaps originally produced in the third century B.C. Of the *Am[postvocalic] ga* eleven are no doubt preserved among the Śvetâmbaras from a late edition of the fifth or sixth century A.D. These works are not written in Sanskrit, but in a popular Prâkrit dialect: for the Jina, like Buddha, used the language of the people when teaching. They contain partly legends about the prophet and his activity as a teacher, partly fragments of a doctrine or attempts at systematic representations of the same. Though the dialect is different they present, in the form of the tales and in the manner of expression, a wonderful resemblance to the sacred writings of the Buddhists. [18] The Digambaras, on the other hand, have preserved nothing of the *Am[postvocalic] ga* but the names. They put in their place later systematic works, also in Prâkrit, and assert, in vindication of their different teaching, that the canon of their rivals is corrupted. In the further course of history, however, both branches of the Jainas have, like the Buddhists, in their continual battles with the Brâhma*n*s, found it necessary to make themselves acquainted with the ancient language of the culture of the latter. First the Digambara and later the Śvetâmbara began to use Sanskrit. They did not rest content with explaining their own teaching in Sanskrit works: they turned also to the secular sciences of the Brâhma*n*s. They have accomplished so much of importance, in grammar, in astronomy, as well as in some branches of letters, that they have won respect even from their enemies, and some of their works are still of importance to European science. In southern India, where they worked among the Dravi*d*ian tribes, they also advanced the development of these languages. The Kanarese literary language and the Tamil and Telugu rest on the foundations laid by the Jaina monks. This activity led them, indeed, far from their proper goal, but it created for them an important position in the history of literature and culture.

The resemblance between the Jainas and the Buddhists, which I have had so often cause to bring forward, suggests the question, whether they are to be regarded as a branch of the latter, or whether they resemble the Buddhists merely because, as their tradition asserts, [19] they sprang from the same period and the same religious movement in opposition to Brâhmanism. This question, was formerly, and is still sometimes, answered in agreement with the first theory, pointing out the undoubted defects in it, to justify the rejection of the Jaina tradition, and even declaring it to be a late and intentional fabrication. In spite of this the second explanation is the right one, because the Buddhists themselves confirm the statements of the Jainas about their prophet. Old historical traditions and inscriptions prove the independent existence of the sect of the Jainas even during the first five centuries after Buddha's death, and among the inscriptions are some which clear the Jaina tradition not only from the suspicion of fraud but bear powerful witness to its honesty. [20]

The oldest canonical books of the Jaina, apart from some

mythological additions and evident exaggerations, contain the following important notes on the life of their last prophet. [21] Vardhamâna was the younger son of Siddhârtha a nobleman who belonged to the Kshatriya race, called in Sanskrit Jñâti or Jñâta, in Prakrit Nâya, and, according to the old custom of the Indian warrior caste, bore the name of a Brâhmanic family the Kâśyapa. His mother, who was called Triśalâ, belonged to the family of the governors of Videha. Siddhârtha's residence was Ku*nd*apura, the Basukund of to-day, a suburb of the wealthy town of Vaiśâlî, the modern Besarh, in Videha or Tirhut. [22] Siddhârtha was son-in-law to the king of Vaiśâlî. Thirty years, it seems, Vardhamâna led a worldly life in his parents' house. He married, and his wife Yaśodâ bore him a daughter Anojjâ, who was married to a noble of the name of Jamâli, and in her turn had a daughter. In his thirty-first year his parents died. As they were followers of Pârśva the twenty-third Jina, they chose, according to the custom of the Jainas, the death of the wise by starvation. Immediately after this Vardhamâna determined to renounce the world. He got permission to take this step from his elder brother Nandivardhana, and the ruler of his land divided his possessions and became a homeless ascetic. He wandered more than twelve years, only resting during the rainy season, in the lands of the Lâ*d*ha, in Vajjabhûmi and Subbhabhûmi, the Rârh of to-day in Bengal, and learned to bear with equanimity great hardships and cruel ill treatment at the hands of the inhabitants of those districts. Besides these he imposed upon himself the severest mortifications; after the first year he discarded clothes and devoted himself to the deepest meditation. In the thirteenth year of this wandering life he believed he had attained to the highest knowledge and to the dignity of a holy one. He then appeared as a prophet, taught the Nirgrantha doctrine, a modification of the religion of Pârśva, and organised the order of the Nirgrantha ascetics. From that time he bore the name of the venerable ascetic Mahâvîra. His career as a teacher lasted not quite thirty years, during which he travelled about, as formerly, all over the country, except during the rainy seasons. He won for himself numerous followers, both of the clergy and the lay class, among whom, however, in the fourteenth year of his period of teaching, a split arose--caused by his son-in-law Jamâli.

The extent of his sphere of influence almost corresponds with that of the kingdoms of Srâvastî or Kosala, Vidcha, Magadha, and Am[postvocalic] ga,--the modern Oudh, and the provinces of Tirhut and Bihâr in Western Bengal. Very frequently he spent the rainy season in his native place Vaiśâlî and in Râjagr iha. Among his contemporaries were, a rival teacher Gosâla the son of Mam[postvocalic] khali--whom he defeated in a dispute, the King of Videha--Bhambhasâra or Bibbhisâra called Sre*n*ika, and his sons Abhayakumâra and the parricide Ajátaśatru or Kû*n*ika, who protected him or accepted his doctrine, and also the nobles of the Lichchhavi and Mallaki races. The town of Pâpâ or Pâvâ, the modern Padraona [23] is given as the place of his death, where he dwelt during the rainy season of the last year of his life, in the house of the scribe of king Hastipâla. Immediately after his death, a second split took place in his community. [24]

On consideration of this information, it immediately strikes one, that the scene of Vardhamâna's activity is laid in the same part of India as Buddha laboured in, and that several of the personalities which play a part in the history of Buddha also appear in the Jaina legend. It is through the kingdoms of Kosala, Videha and Magadha, that Buddha is said to have wandered preaching, and their capitals Śrâvastî and Râjagr iha are just the places named, where he founded the largest communities. It is also told of the inhabitants of Vaiśâlî that many turned to his doctrine. Many legends are told of his intercourse and friendship with Bimbisâra or Śre*n*ika, king of Videha, also of the murder of the latter by his son Ajâtaśatru, who, tortured with remorse, afterwards approached Buddha; mention is also made of his brother Abhayakumâra, likewise Makkhali Gosâla is mentioned among Buddha's opponents and rivals. It is thus clear that the oldest Jaina legend makes Vardhamâna a fellow countryman and contemporary of Buddha, and search might be suggested in the writings of the Buddhists for confirmation of these assumptions. Such indeed are to be found in no small number.

Even the oldest works of the Singalese Canon,--which date apparently from the beginning of the second century after Buddha's death, or the fourth century B.C., and which at any rate had their final edition in the third,--frequently mention an opposing sect of ascetics, the Nigan *t*ha, which the northern texts, written in Sanskrit, recognise among the opponents of Buddha, under the name Nirgrantha, whom an old *Sûtra* [25] describes as "heads of companies of disciples and students, teachers of students, well known, renowned, founders of schools of doctrine, esteemed as good men by the multitude". Their leader is also named; he is called in Pâli Nâtaputta, in Sanskrit Jñâtiputra, that is the son of Jñâti or Nâta. The similarity between these words and the names of the family Jñâti, Jñâta or Naya, to which Vardhamâna belonged is apparent. Now since in older Buddhist literature, the title 'the son of the man of the family N. N.' is very often used instead of the individual's name, as for example, 'the son of the Sâkiya' is put for Buddha-Sâkiyaputta, so that it is difficult not to suppose that Nâtaputta or Jñâtiputra, the leader of the Niga*nt*ha or Nirgrantha sect, is the same person as Vardhamâna, the descendant of the Jñâti family and founder of the Nirgrantha or Jaina sect. If we follow up this idea, and gather together the different remarks of the Buddhists about the opponents of Buddha, then it is apparent that his identity with Vardhamâna is certain. A number of rules of doctrine are ascribed to him, which are also found among the Jainas, and some events in his life, which we have already found in the accounts of the life of Vardhamâna, are related.

In one place in the oldest part of the Singalese canon, the assertion is put into the mouth of Niga*nt*ha Nâtaputta, that the *Kiriyâvâda*--the doctrine of activity, separates his system from Buddha's teaching. We shall certainly recognise in this doctrine, the rule of the *Kiriyâ*, the activity of souls, upon which Jainism places so great importance. [26] Two other rules from the doctrine of souls are quoted in a later work, not canonical: there it is stated, in a collection of false doctrines which Buddha's rivals taught, that Niga*nt*ha asserts that cold water was living. Little drops of water contained small souls, large drops, large souls. Therefore he forbade his followers, the use of cold water. It is not difficult, in these curious rules to recognise the Jaina dogma, which asserts the existence of souls, even in the mass of lifeless elements of earth, water, fire, and wind. This also proves, that the Niga*nt*ha admitted the classification of souls, so often ridiculed by the Brâhma*n*s, which distinguishes between great and small. This work, like others, ascribes to Nigan*t*ha the assertion, that the so-called three *dan d a*--the three instruments by which man can cause injury to creatures--thought, word, and body, are separate active causes of sin. The Jaina doctrine agrees also in this case, which always specially represents the three and prescribes for each a special control. [27]

Besides these rules, which perfectly agree with one another, there are still two doctrines of the Niga*nt*ha to be referred to which seem to, or really do, contradict the Jainas; namely, it is stated that Nâtaputta demanded from his disciples the taking of four, not as in Vardhamâna's case, of five great vows. Although this difficulty may seem very important at first glance, it is, however, set aside by an oft repeated assertion in the Jaina works. They repeatedly say that Pàrśva, the twenty-third Jina only recognised four vows, and Vardhamâna added the fifth. The Buddhists have therefore handed down a dogma which Jainism recognises. The question is merely whether they or the Jainas are the more to be trusted. If the latter, and it is accepted that Vardhamâna was merely the reformer of an old religion, then the Buddhists must be taxed with an easily possible confusion between the earlier and later teachers. If, on the other hand, the Jaina accounts of their twenty-third prophet are regarded as mythical, and Vardhamâna is looked upon as the true founder of the sect,--then the doctrine of the four vows must be ascribed to the latter, and we must accept as a fact that he had changed his views on this point. In any case, however, the Buddhist statement speaks for, rather than against, the identity of Niga*nt*ha with Jina. [28]

Vardhamâna's system, on the other hand, is quite irreconcilable with Nâtaputta's assertion that virtue as well as sin, happiness as well as unhappiness is unalterably fixed for men by fate, and nothing in their destiny can be altered by the carrying out of the holy law. It is, however, just as irreconcilable with the other Buddhist accounts of the teaching of their opponent; because it is absolutely unimaginable, that the same man, who lays vows upon his followers, the object of which is to avoid sin, could nevertheless make virtue and sin purely dependent upon the disposition of fate, and preach the uselessness of carrying out the law. The accusation that Nâtaputta embraced fatalism must therefore be regarded as an invention and an outcome of sect hatred as well as of the wish to throw discredit on their opponents. [29]

The Buddhist remarks on the personality and life of Nâtaputta are still more remarkable. They say repeatedly that he laid claim to the dignity of an Arhat and to omniscience which the Jainas also claim for their prophet, whom they prefer simply to call 'the Arhat' and who possesses the universe-embracing '*Kevala*' knowledge. [30] A history of conversions, tells us further that Nâtaputta and his disciples disdained to cover their bodies; we are told just the same of Vardhamâna. [31] A story in the oldest part of the Singalese canon gives an interesting and important instance of his activity in teaching. Buddha, so the legend runs, once came to the town Vaiśâlî, the seat of the Kshatriya of the Lichchhavi race. His name, his law, his community were highly praised by the nobles of the Lichchhavi in the senate-house. Sîha, their general, who was a follower of the Niga*nt*ha, became anxious to know the great teacher. He went to his master Nâtaputta, who happened to be staying in Vaiśâlî just then, and asked permission to pay the visit. Twice Nâtaputta refused him. Then Sîha determined to disobey him. He sought Buddha out, heard his teaching and was converted by him. In order to show his attachment to his new teacher he invited Buddha and his disciples to eat with him. On the acceptance of the invitation, Sîha commanded his servants to provide flesh in honour of the occasion. This fact came to the ears of the followers of the Niga*nt*ha. Glad to have found an occasion to damage Buddha, they hurried in great numbers through the town, crying out, that Sîha had caused a great ox to be killed for Buddha's entertainment; that Buddha had eaten of the flesh of the animal although he knew it had been killed on his account, and was, therefore guilty of the death of the animal. The accusation was brought to Siha's notice and was declared by him to be a calumny. Buddha, however preached a sermon after the meal, in which he forbade his disciples to partake of the flesh of such animals as had been killed on their account. The legend also corroborates the account in the Jaina works, according to which Vardhamâna often resided in Vaiśâlî and had a strong following in that town. It is probably related to show that his sect was stricter, as regards the eating of flesh, than the Buddhists, a point, which again agrees with the statutes of the Jainas. [32]

The account of Nâtaputta's death is still more important. "Thus I heard it", says an old book of the Singalese canon, the *Sâmagâma Sutta*, "once the Venerable one lived in Sâmagâma in the land of the Sâkya. At that time, however, certainly the Niga*nt*ha Nâtaputta had died in Pâvâ. After his death the Niga*nt*ha wandered about disunited, separate, quarrelling, fighting, wounding each other with words." [33] Here we have complete confirmation of the statement of the Jaina canon as to the place where Vardhamâna entered *Nirvân a*, as well as of the statement that a schism occurred immediately after his death.

The harmony between the Buddhist and Jaina tradition, as to the person of the head of the Nirgrantha is meanwhile imperfect. It is disturbed by the description of Nâtaputta as a member of the Brâhmanic sect of the Âgniveśyâyana, whilst Vardhamâna belonged to the Kâśyapa. The point is however so insignificant, that an error on the part of the Buddhists is easily possible. [34] It is quite to be understood that perfect exactness is not to be expected among the Buddhists or any other sect in describing the person of a hated enemy. Enmity and scorn, always present, forbid that. The most that one can expect is that the majority and most important of the facts given may agree.

This condition is undoubtedly fulfilled in the case on hand. It cannot, therefore be denied, that, in spite of this difference, in spite also of the absurdity of one article of the creed ascribed to him, Vardhamâna Jñâtiputra, the founder of the Nirgrantha--or Jaina community is none other than Buddha's rival. From Buddhist accounts in their canonical works as well as in other books, it may be seen that this rival was a dangerous and influential one, and that even in Buddha's time his teaching had spread considerably. Their legends about conversions from other sects very often make mention of Nirgrantha sectarians, whom Buddha's teaching or that of his disciples had alienated from their faith. Also they say in their descriptions of other rivals of Buddha, that these, in order to gain esteem, copied the Nirgrantha and went unclothed, or that they were looked upon by the people as Nirgrantha holy ones, because they happened to have lost their clothes. Such expressions would be inexplicable if Vardhamâna's community had not become of great importance. [35]

This agrees with several remarks in the Buddhist chronicles, which assert the existence of the Jainas in different districts of India during the first century after Buddha's death. In the memoirs of the Chinese Buddhist and pilgrim Hiuen Tsiang, who visited India in the beginning of the seventh century of our era, is to be found an extract from the ancient annals of Magadha, which proves the existence of the Nirgrantha or Jainas in their original home from a very early time. [36] This extract relates to the building of the great monastry at Nâlandâ, the high school of Buddhism in eastern India, which was founded shortly after Buddha's *Nirvân a*, and mentions incidentally that a Nirgrantha who was a great astrologer and prophet had prophesied the future success of the new building. At almost as early a period the *Mahâvan[g]sa*, composed in the fifth century A.D., fixes the appearance of the Nirgrantha in the island of Ceylon. It is said that the king Pa*nd*ukâbhaya, who ruled in the beginning of the second century after Buddha, from 367-307 B.C. built a temple and a monastery for two Nirgranthas. The monastery is again mentioned in the same work in the account of the reign of a later king Va*tt*âgâmini, cir. 38-10 B.C. It is related that Va*tt*âgâmini being offended by the inhabitants, caused it to be destroyed after it had existed during the reigns of twenty one kings, and erected a Buddhist Sam[postvocalic] ghârâma in its place. The latter piece of information is found also in the *Dîpavan[g]sa* of more than a century earlier. [37]

None of these works can indeed be looked upon as a truly historical source. There are, even in those paragraphs which treat of the oldest history after Buddha's death, proofs enough that they simply hand down a faulty historical tradition. In spite of this, their statements on the Nirgrantha, cannot be denied a certain weight, because they are closely connected on the one side with the Buddhist canon, and on the other they agree with the indisputable sources of history, which relate to a slightly later period.

The first authentic information on Vardhamâna's sect is given by our oldest inscriptions, the religious edicts of the Maurya king

Aśoka, who, according to tradition was anointed in the year 219 after Buddha's death, and--as the reference to his Grecian contemporaries, Antiochos, Magas, Alexander, Ptolemaeus and Antigonas confirms,--ruled, during the second half of the third century B.C. over the whole of India with the exception of the Dekhan. This prince interested himself not only in Buddhism, which he professed in his later years, but he took care, in a fatherly way, as he repeatedly relates, of all other religious sects in his vast kingdom. In the fourteenth year of his reign, he appointed officials, called law-superintendents, whose duty it was to watch over the life of the different communities, to settle their quarrels, to control the distribution of their legacies and pious gifts. He says of them in the second part of the seventh 'pillar' edict, which he issued in the twenty-ninth year of his reign, "My superintendents are occupied with various charitable matters, they are also engaged with all sects of ascetics and householders; I have so arranged that they will also be occupied with the affairs of the *Sam[postvocalic] gha*; likewise I have arranged that they will be occupied with the Âjîvika Brâhma*n*s; I have arranged it that they will also be occupied with the Niga*nt*ha". [38] The word *Sam[postvocalic] gha* serves here as usual for the Buddhist monks. The Âjívikas, whose name completely disappears later, are often named in the sacred writings of the Buddhists and the Jainas as an influential sect. They enjoyed the special favour of Aśoka, who, as other inscriptions testify, caused several caves at Baràbar to be made into dwellings for their ascetics. [39] As in the still older writings of the Buddhist canon, the name Niga*nt*ha here can refer only to the followers of Vardhamâna. As they are here, along with the other two favourites, counted worthy of special mention, we may certainly conclude that they were of no small importance at the time. Had they been without influence and of small numbers Aśoka would hardly have known of them, or at least would not have singled them out from the other numerous nameless sects of which he often speaks. It may also be supposed that they were specially numerous in their old home, as Aśoka's capital Pâ*t*aliputra lay in this land. Whether they spread far over these boundaries, cannot be ascertained.

On the other hand we possess two documents from the middle of the next century which prove that they advanced into south-eastern

India as far as Kalim[postvocalic] ga. These are the inscriptions at Kha*nd*agiri in Orissa, of the great King Khâravela and his first wife, who governed the east coast of India from the year 152 to 165 of the Maurya era that is, in the first half of second century B.C.

The larger inscription, unfortunately very much disfigured, contains an account of the life of Khâravela from his childhood till the thirteenth year of his reign. It begins with an appeal to the Arhat and Siddha, which corresponds to the beginning of the five-fold form of homage still used among the Jainas, and mentions the building of temples in honour of the Arhat as well as an image of the first Jina, which was taken away by a hostile king. The second and smaller inscription asserts that Khâravela's wife caused a cave to be prepared for the ascetics of Kalinga, "who believed on the Arhat." [40]

From a somewhat later period, as the characters show, from the first century B.C. comes a dedicatory inscription which has been found far to the west of the original home of the Jainas, in Mathurà on the Jamnâ. It tells of the erection of a small temple in honour of the Arhat Vardhamâna, also of the dedication of seats for the teachers, a cistern, and a stone table. The little temple, it says, stood beside the temple of the guild of tradesmen, and this remark proves, that Mathurâ, which, according to the tradition of the Jainas, was one of the chief scats of their religion, possessed a community of Jainas even before the time of this inscription. [41]

A large member of dedicatory inscriptions have come to light, which are dated from the year 5 to 98 of the era of the Indo-Skythian kings, Kanishka, Huvishka, and Vâsudeva (Bazodeo) and therefore belong at latest to the end of the first and to the second century A.D. They are all on the pedestals of statues, which are recognisable partly by the special mention of the names of Vardhamâna and the Arhat Mahâvíra, partly by absolute nudity and other marks. They show, that the Jaina community continued to flourish in Mathurâ and give besides extraordinarily important information, as I found in a renewed research into the ancient history of the sect. In a number of them, the dedicators of the statues give not only their own names, but also those of the religious teachers to whose communities they belonged. Further, they give these teachers their official titles, still used among the Jainas: *vâchaka*, 'teacher', and *gan in*, 'head of a school'. Lastly they specify the names of the schools to which the teachers belonged, and those of their subdivisions. The schools are called, *gan a*, 'companies'; the subdivisions, *kula*, 'families' and *śâkhà*, 'branches'. Exactly the same division into *gan a, śâkhà*, and *kula* is found in a list in one of the canonical works, of the Śvetâmbaras, the *Kalpasûtra*, which gives the number of the patriarchs and of the schools founded by them, and it is of the highest importance, that, in spite of mutilation and faulty reproduction of the inscriptions, nine of the names, which appear in the *Kalpasûtra* are recognisable in them, of which part agree exactly, part, through the fault of the stone-mason or wrong reading by the copyist, are somewhat defaced. According to the *Kalpasûtra*, Sushita, the ninth successor to Vardhamâna In the position of patriarch, together with his companion Supratibuddha, founded the 'Ko*d*iya' or 'Kautika *gan a*, which split up into four '*sâkhà*, and four '*kula*'. Inscription No. 4. which is dated in the year 9 of the king Kanishka or 87. A.D. (?) gives us a somewhat ancient form of the name of the *gan a Kot iya* and that of one of its branches exactly corresponding to the *Vairi śàkhâ.* Mutilated or wrongly written, the first word occurs also in inscriptions Nos. 2, 6 and 9 as *koto-, ket t iya*, and *ka* ..., the second in No. 6 as *Vorâ*. One of the families of this *gan a*, the *Vân iya kula* is mentioned in No. 6, and perhaps in No. 4. The name of a second, the *Praśnavàhan aka*, seems to have appeared in No. 19. The last inscription mentions also another branch of the Kot iya gan a, the *Majhimâ sâkhâ*, which, according to the *Kalpasûtra,* was founded by Priyagantha the second disciple of Susthita. Two still older schools which, according to tradition, sprang from the fourth disciple of the eighth patriarch, along with some of their divisions appear in inscriptions Nos. 20 and 10. These are the *Aryya-Udehikîya gan a*, called the school of the Ârya-Roha*n*a in the *Kalpasûtra*, to which belonged the *Parihâsaka kula* and the *Pûrnapâtrikâ śâkhâ,* as also the *Charân a gan a* with the *Prîtidharmika kula.* Each of these names is, however, somewhat mutilated by one or more errata in writing. [42] The statements in the inscriptions about the teachers and their schools are of no small importance in themselves for the history of the Jainas. If, at the end of the first century A.D.(?) many separate schools of Jaina ascetics existed, a great age and lively activity, as well as great care as regards the traditions of the sect, may be inferred. The agreement of the inscriptions with the *Kalpasûtra* leads still further however: it proves on the one side that the Jainas of Mathurâ were Śvetâmbara, and that the schism, which split the sect into two rival branches occurred long before the beginning of our era. On the other hand it proves that the tradition of the Svetâmbara really contains ancient historic elements, and by no means deserves to be looked upon with distrust. It is quite probable that, like all traditions, it is not altogether free from error. But it can no longer be declared to be the result of a later intentional misrepresentation, made in order to conceal the dependence of Jainism on Buddhism. It is no longer possible to dispute its authenticity with regard to those points which are confirmed by independent statements of other sects, and to assert, for example, that the Jaina account of the life of Vardhamâna, which agrees with the statements of the Buddists, proves nothing as regards the age of Jainism because in the late fixing of the canon of the Śvetâmbaras in the sixth century after Christ it may have been drawn from Buddhist works. Such an assertion which, under all circumstances, is a bold one, becomes entirely untenable when it is found that the tradition in question states correctly facts which lie not quite three centuries distant from Vardhamâna's time, and that the sect, long before the first century of our era kept strict account of their internal affairs. [43]

Unfortunately the testimony to the ancient history of the Jainas, so far as made known by means of inscriptions, terminates here. Interesting as it would be to follow the traces of their communities in the later inscriptions, which become so numerous from the fifth century A.D. onwards and in the description of his travels by Hiuen Tsiang, who found them spread through the whole of India and even beyond its boundaries, it would be apart from our purpose. The documents quoted suffice, however, to confirm the assertion that during the first five centuries after Buddha's death both the statements of Buddhist tradition and real historical sources give evidence to the existence of the Jainas as an important religious community independent of Buddhism, and that there are among the historical sources some which entirely clear away the suspicion that the tradition of the Jainas themselves is intentionally falsified.

The advantage gained for Indian history from the conclusion that Jainism and Buddhism are two contemporary sects--having arisen in the same district,--is no small one. First, this conclusion shows that the religious movement of the sixth and fifth centuries B.C. in eastern India must have been a profound one. If not only one, but certainly two, and perhaps more reformers, appeared at the same time, preaching teachers, who opposed the existing circumstances in the same manner, and each of whom gained no small number of followers for their doctrines, the desire to overthrow the Brahmanical order of things must have been generally and deeply felt. This conclusion shows then that the transformation of the religious life in India was not merely the work of a religious community. Many strove to attain this object although separated from one another. It is now recognisable, though preliminarily, in one point only, that the religious history of India from the fifth century B.C. to the eighth or ninth A.D. was not made up of the fight between Brahmanism and Buddhism alone. This conclusion allows us, lastly, to hope that the thorough investigation of the oldest writings of the Jainas and their relations with Buddhism on the one hand and with Brahmanism on the other will afford many important ways of access to a more exact knowledge concerning the religious ideas which prevailed in the sixth and fifth centuries B.C., and to the establishment of the boundaries of originality between the different systems.

APPENDIX A.

Copies of the mutilated inscriptions referred to, were published by General Sir A. Cunningham in his *Archaeological Survey Reports*, vol. III, plates xiii-xv. Unfortunately they have been presented from 'copies' and are therefore full of errors, which are due for the most part, doubtless, to the copyist and not to the sculptor. It is not difficult, however, in most cases under consideration here, to restore the correct reading. Usually only vowel signs are omitted or misread and, here, and there, consonants closely resembling one another as *va* and *cha, va*, and *dha, ga* and *śa, la* and *na* are interchanged.

The formulae of the inscriptions are almost universally the same. First comes the date, then follows the name of a reverend teacher, next, the mention of the school and the subdivision of it to which he belonged. Then the persons, who dedicated the statues are named (mostly women), and who belonged to the community of the said teacher. The description of the gift forms the conclusion. The dialect of the inscriptions shows that curious mixture of Sanskr ĭt and Prâkr ĭt which is found in almost all documents of the Indo-Skythian kings, and whichas Dr. Hoernle was the first to recognise--was one of the literary languages of northern and northwestern India during the first centuries before and after the commencement of our era.

In the calculation of dates, I use the favourite starting point for the era of the Indo-Skythian kings, which unfortunately, is not certainly determined, and assume that it is identical with the *Saka* era of 78-¼ A.D. The rule of these princes could not have fallen later: in my opinion it was somewhat earlier [44] I give here transcripts and restorations of such inscriptions as mention Jaina schools or titles.

1. The inscription which is the most important for my purpose and at the same time one of the best preserved, is Sir A. Cunningham's No. 6, plate xiii, which was found on the base of a Jaina image (*Arch. Sur. Rep.* vol. III, p. 31). The copy compared with a rubbing gives the following reading, (the letters within parentheses are damaged):

L. 1. *Siddham[postvocalic] sam[postvocalic] 20 gramâ 1 di 10 + 5 ko(t i)yato gan ato (Vâ)n iyato kulato V(ai)r(i)to śâkâto Śirikâto*

2. *(bha)ttito vâchakasya Aryya-Sam[postvocalic] ghasihasya nir(v)varttanam[postvocalic] Dattilasya.... Vi.-*

3. *lasya ko(t hu)bi(ki)ya Jayavâlasya Devadâsasya Nâgadinasya cha Nâgadinâye cha (mâ)tu.*

4. *śrâ(vi)kâye (D)i-*

5. *(nâ)ye dânam[postvocalic] . i*

6. *Varddhamâna pra-*

7. *timâ|*

The lacuna in line 2, after *Dattilasya*, probably contained the word *duhituye* or *dhûtuye* and part of a male name of which only the letter *vi* is visible. In l. 3, possibly *kot habiniye* is to be read instead of *kot hubikiye*. As there is room for one more letter at the end of the line, I propose to read *mâtuye*. In l. 5, *Dinâye* would stand for *Dattâyâh[postvocalic]* and be the genitive of a female name *Dinnâ* or *Dattâ*, which has been shortened *bhâmâvat*. There can be no doubt that the word *śrî*, or *śiri*, which is required, has stood before *Vardhamâna*. With these restorations the translation is as follows:

"Success! The year 20, summer (*month*) I, day 15. An image of glorious Vardhamâna, the gift of the female lay-disciple Dinâ [*i.e.* Dinnâ or Dattâ] , the [*daughter*] of Attila, the wife of Vi..la, the mother of Jayavâla [Jayapâla] , of Devadâsa and Nâgadina [*i. e.* Nâgadinna or Nâgadatta] and of Nâgadina [*i.e.* of Nâgadinnâ or Nâgadattâ] --(*this statue being*) the *nirvartana* [45] of the preacher Aryya-Sam[postvocalic] ghasiha [*i.e.* Ârya-Sam[postvocalic] ghasim[postvocalic] ha] , out of the Ko*t*iya school, the Vâniya race, the Vairi branch, the Śirikâ division".

The inscription given *Arch. Sur. Rep.* vol. XX, plate v, No. 6 reads, according to an excellent rubbing:

L. 1. *Namo Araham[postvocalic] tânain namo Siddhâna sam[postvocalic]* 60 [46] + 2

2. *gra 3 di 5 etâye purvâye Râkarasya Aryakakasaghastasya*

3. *śishyâ Âtapikogahabaryasya nirvartana chatnuvarnasya sam[postvocalic] ghasya*

4. *yâ dinnâ pat ibhâ[bho?] ga* 1 (?) | (?) *Vaihikâya datti*|

"Adoration to the Arhats, adoration to the Siddhas! The year 62, the summer (*month*) 3, the day 5; on the above date a *yâ.* was given to the community, which includes four classes, as an enjoyment (*or* one share for each) (*this being*) the *nirvartana* of Atapikogahabarya, the pupil of Arya-Kakasaghasta (Ârya-Karkaśagharshita), a native of Rârâ (Râ*d*hâ). The gift of Vaihikâ (*or*, Vaihitâ)."

2. With the inscription No. 6 of the year 20, No. 4 (plate xiii) agrees; it was also found on a Jaina pedestal. With better readings from a rubbing of the first side only, I propose for the other portions, of which I have no rubbings, the following emendations,--l. 1, *Vâniyato kulato, sâkhâto*; l. 2, *kut umbimye;* I also note that the lacuna in line 2, 3th and 4th sides, would be filled exactly by *ye śrî-Vardhamânasya pratimâ kâritâ sarvasattvâ.* The former existence of the first and last seven letters may be considered certain. My restoration of the whole is,--

L. 1 (1st side) *Siddham[postvocalic] mahârâjasya Kanishkasya râjye sam[postvocalic] vatsare navame* [47] (2nd side).. *mâsc pratha* 1 *divase* 5 *a-(3rd) [syâm[postvocalic]] purvv[â]ye Kot iyato gan ato Vâniya[to]* (4th) *[ku] lato Vairito śâkâto vâchaka-*

2. (1st side) *[sya] [N]âganam[postvocalic] disa ni[rva]r[ta]nam[postvocalic] Brah[ma] ... [dhû-(2nd)tuye] Bhat t umitasa kut u[m[postvocalic]]bi[n]i[ye] Vikat â-(3rd)[ye śrî Vardhamânasya pratimâ kâritâ sarva-*(4th) *satvâ] nam[postvocalic] hita-*

3. *[sukhâye]* ;

and the translation:--

"Success! During the reign of the great king Kanishka, in the ninth year, 9, in the first month, 1, of ..., on the day 5,--on the above date [an image of glorious Vardhamâna has been caused to be made] for the welfare [and happiness] of [all created beings] by Vikatâ, the house-wife of Bha*tt*imita (Bhat*t*imitra) and [daughter of] Brâhma ...--(this statue being) the *nirvartana* of the preacher Nâganam[postvocalic] idi, out of the Ko*t*iya school (*gan a*), the Vâ*n*iya line (*kula*), (and) the Vairi branch (*śâkhâ*)."

If we now turn to the *Kalpasûtra*, we find that Su*tt*hiya or Susthita, the eighth successor of Vardhamâna, founded the Kau*t*ika or Ko*d*iya ga*n*a, which split up into four śâkhâs and four kulas. The third of the former was the Vajrî or Vairî, and the third of the latter was the Vâ*n*îya or Vâ*n*ijja. It is evident that the names of the *gan a, kula*, and *śâkhâ* agree with those mentioned in the two inscriptions, Ko*t*iya being a somewhat older form of Ko*d*iya. But it is interesting to note that the further subdivision of the Vairî śâkhâ--the Śirikâ bhatti (Srikâ bhakti) which inscription No. 6 mentions, is not known to the *Kalpasûtra*. This is a gap such as may by be expected to occur in a list handed down by oral tradition.

3. The Ko*t*ika ga*n*a is again mentioned in the badly mutilated inscription No. 19, plate xv. A complete restoration is impossible.

L. 1. *Sam[postvocalic] valsare 90 va...sya kut ubani. vadânasya vodhuya...*

2. *K|ot iyato| gan ato |Praśna|vâha|na|kato kulato Majhamâto śâkhâto...sa nikâye bhati gâlâe thabâni...*

It may, however, be inferred from the fragments of the first line that the dedication was made by a woman who was described as the wife (*kut umbinî*) of one person and as the daughter-in-law (*vadhu*) of another. The first part of line 2, restored as above gives--"in the congregation of ... out of the Ko*t*iya school, the

Praśnavâhanaka line and the Majhamâ branch...." The restoration of the two names Kotiya and Praśnavâhanaka seems to me absolutely certain, because they exactly fill the blanks in the inscription, and because the information in the *Kalpasûtra* (S. B. E. vol. XXII, p. 293) regarding the Madhyamâśâkhâ points in that direction. The latter work tells us that Priyagantha, the second pupil of Susthita and Supratibuddha, founded a śâkhâ, called Madhyamâ or Majhimâ.

As our inscriptions show that Professor Jacobi's explanation of the terms *gan a, kula* and *śâkhâ* [48] is correct and that the first denotes the school, the second the line of teachers, and the third a branch which separated from such a line, it follows that the śâkhâs named in the *Kalpasûtra* without the mention of a *gan a* and *kula*, must belong to the last preceding *gan a* and derive their origin from one of its *kulas*. Hence the Madhyamâ śâkhâ doubtless was included in the Kautika gana, and an offshoot of one of its *kulas*, the fourth of which is called Praśnavâhanaka or Panhavâhanaya. The correctness of these inferences is proved by Râjaśckhara's statement regarding his spiritual descent at the end of the *Prabandha kosha*, which he composed in Vik. sam[postvocalic] 1405. He informs us that he belonged to the Kotika gana, the Praśnavâhana kula, the Madhyamâ śâkhâ, the Harshapurîya gachha and the Maladhâri samtâna, founded by the illustrious Abhayasûri.

For the last words of l. 2 I do not dare to propose an emendation; I merely note that the gift seems to have consisted of pillars, *thabâni*, i. e. *stambhâh[postvocalic]*.

4. The Kotiya gana seems finally to be mentioned in pl. xiii, No. 2, where the copy of line 1, 2nd side may be corrected as,--

Siddha--sa 5 he 1 di 10 + 2 asyâ purvvâye Kot (iya).

5. Names of an older *gan a* and of one of its *kulas* occur in No. 10 plate xiv, where the copy, which is faulty, may allow the following partial restoration,---

L. 1. *Sa 40 + 7 gra 2 di 20 etasyâ purvvâye Vâran e gan e Petidhamikakulavâchakasya Rohanadisya sîsasya Senasya nivatanam sâvaka-Da*

2. *...pashân avadhaya Giha..ka.bha.. prapâ [di] nâ..mâ ta...*

which I translate--

"The year 47, the summer (month) 2, the day 20,--on the above date a drinking fountain was given by ..., the ... of the lay-disciple Da ... (this being) the *nivatana* of Sena the pupil of Rohanadi (Rohanandi) and preacher of the Petidhamika (Praitidharmika) line, in the Vâra*n*a school."

Varane must be a mistake for the very similar word *Chârane*. The second *kula* of this *gan a* which, according to the *Kalpasûtra* (*S.B.E*. vol. XXII, p. 291) was founded by Śrîgupta, the fifth pupil of Ârya Suhastin, is the Prîtidharmika (p. 292). It is easy to see that a similar name is hidden in the compound *Petivamikakutavâchakasya* 'of the preacher of the Petivâmika line'; and an inscription excavated by Dr. Fuhrer at Mathurâ mentions the Petivâmika (*kula*) of the Vârana *gan a*. With the second line little can be done: if the letters *prapâ* are correct and form a word, one of the objects dedicated must have been a drinking fountain.

6. The inscription No. 20, plate xv offers likewise slightly corrupt and mutilated names of a *gan a*, a *kula* and a *sâkhâ*, mentioned in the *Kalpasûtra*. In the lithographed copy lines 3-7 are hopeless and there is no rubbing to help. The word *thitu* 'of a daughter' in line 6, and the following *ma.uya* which is probably a misreading of *mâtuye* 'of the mother' show that this dedication also was made by a female. The last four syllables *vato maho* are probably the remnant of another namaskâra--*namo bhagavato Mahâvîrasya*. As regards the proper names, Aryya Rehiniya is an impossible form; but on comparison with the next inscription to be mentioned, it is evident that the stone must have read *Aryvodchikiyâto* or *Aryyadehikiyâto g>n â[to]* . [49] According to the *Kalpasûtra* (*S.B.E*. vol. XXII, p. 291) Ârya-Roha*n*a was the first pupil of Ârya Suhastin and founded the Uddeha ga*n*a. The latter split up into four śâkhâs and into six kulas. The name of its fourth śâkhâ, Pûr*n*apatrikâ, closely resembles--especially in its consonantal elements--that of the inscription, *Petaputrikâ*, and I do not hesitate in correcting the latter to *Ponapatrikâ* which would be the equivalent of Sansk.

Paur*n*apatrikâ. Among the six kulas is the Parihâsaka, and considering the other agreements, I believe it probable that the mutilated name read as *Puridha.ka* is a misreading of *Parihâka*, We may emend the first two times and read as follows,--

L. 1. *Siddha|m| namo arahato Mahâvir|a|sya devanâśasya | râjña Vâsudevasya sam[postvocalic] vatsare 90 + 8 varshamâse + divase 10 | 1 etasyâ.*

2. *purvv|â|y|e| Aryyo-D|e|h|i|kiyâto gan â[|to| P|a|vi|hâsa|k|a|kula|to| P|ou|ap|a|trikât|o| śâkâto gan |i|sya Aryya-Devadatta|sya| na... ...*

3. *ryya-Kshemasya*

4. *prakagirin e*

5. *kihadiye prajâ*

6. *tasya Pravarakasya dhitu Varan asya gatvakasya ma|t|uya Mitra(?)sa ...datta gâ*

7. *ye..|namo bhaga|vato mah|âvîrasya|*

and the translation (so far) will be,--

> "Success! Adoration to the Arhat Mahâvirâ, the destroyer(?) of the gods. In the year of king Vâsudeva, 98, in the month 4 of the rainy season, on the day 11--on the above date ... of the chief of the school (*gan in*) Aryya-Devadata (Devadatta) out of the school (*gan a*) of the Aryya-Udehikîya (Ârya-Uddehikiya), out of the Parihâsaka line (*kula*), out of the Ponapatrikâ (Paur*n*apatrikâ) branch (*śâkhâ*)." [50]

These and many other statements in the inscriptions, about the teachers and their schools are of no small importance in themselves for the early history of the Jainas. The agreement of the above with the *Kalpasûtra* can best be shown by placing the statements in question against one another. The inscriptions prove the actual existence of twenty of the subdivisions mentioned in the Sthavirâvali of the *Kalpasûtra*. Among its eight ga*n*as we can certainly trace three, possibly four--the Uddchika, Vâra*n*a, Veśavâ*d*iya(?) and Ko*d*iya.

Inscriptions:

1. Ko*tt*iya (Ko*d*iya)
Gana

.. . .

Bramadâsika kula	
Thâniya kula	Uchchenâgarî śâkhâ
P[a*n*ha] vahu[*n*aya] ku[la]	Vairî, Vairiyâ śâkhâ
Majhamâ śâkhâ	

The Sthavirâvalî of the *Kalpasûtra (Sac. Bks. of the East*, vol. XXII, p. 292) states that Sus*t*hita and Supratibuddha founded the--

Ko*t*iya or
Kau*t*aka
Ga*n*a

.. . .

kulas	**śâkhâs**
1. *Bambhalijja*	1. *Uchchanâgarî*
2. Vachchhalijja	2. *Vijjâharî*
3. *Vân îya* or *Vân îjja*	3. Vajrî
4. Panhavâhanaya	4. *Majjhimáka* or Praśnavâhanaka
	5. Majjhîma (scholar of the two teachers. founded by Priyagantha the second)

Inscriptions:

2. Vâra*n*a Ga*n*a

.. . .

kulas

Petivamika

Ârуya Hâtikiya

Puśyamitrîya

Aryya-Chetiya

Kaniyasika

śâkhâs

Vâjanâgarî

Harîtamâlakadhî

The *Kalpasûtra* states that Śrîgupta of the Hâritagotra founded the Châra*n*a ga*n*a, which was divided into four *śâkhâs* and into seven *kulas*:

Châra*n*a-ga*n*a

.. . .

kulas

1. Vachchhalijja
2. *Pîdhammiya*
3. *Hâlijja*
4. *Pûsamittijja*
5. Mâlijja
6. *Ârya-Ched aya*
7. *Kan hasaha*

śâkhâs

Sam[postvocalic] kâśikâ

Vajjanâgarî

Gavedhukâ

Hâriyamâlagârî

Inscriptions:

:

3. Aryya-Udekiya Ga*n*a

.. . .

kulas

Nágabhatikiya

Puridha

Petaputrikâ śâkhâ

The *Kalpasûtra* says Ârya-Rohana of the Kâśyapa gotra founded the

Uddeha

Gana

.. . .

kulas	
1. *Nâgabhûya*	Udumbarijjiyâ
2. Somabhûta	Mâsapûrikâ
3. Ullagachchha (or Ârdrakachchha?)	Matipatrikâ
4. Ilatthilijja	*Pun n apattiyâ*
5. Nandijja	
6. *Parihâsaka*	

Inscriptions:

4. [Veśavâdiya Ga*n*a] [51]

.

[Me] hika kula

The *Kalpasûtra*:--Kâmarddhi of the Ku*nd*alagotra founded the Veśavâ*t*ika ga*n*a which was divided into four śàkhâs, and into four kulas:--

Veśavâ*t*ika Ga*n*a

.. . .

kulas	**śâkhâs**
Ga*n*ika	Śrâvastikâ
Maighika	Rajjapâliyâ
Kâmarddhika	Antarijjiyâ
Indrapuraka	Khemalijjiyâ

[52]

The resemblance of most of these names is so complete that no explanation is necessary.

The Indian Sect of the Jains

FOOTNOTES

Footnote 1: In notes on the Jainas, one often finds the view expressed, that the *Digambaras* belong only to the south, and the *Śvetâmbaras* to the north. This is by no means the case. The former in the Panjâb, in eastern Râjputâna and in the North West Provinces, are just as numerous, if not more so, than the latter, and also appear here and there in western Râjputâna and Gujarât: see *Indian Antiquary*, vol. VII, p. 28.

Footnote 2: The ascetics of lower rank, now called Pa*nd*it, now-a-days wear the costume of the country. The Bha*tt*âraka, the heads of the sect, usually wrap themselves in a large cloth (*chadr*). They lay it off during meals. A disciple then rings a bell as a sign that entrance is forbidden (*Ind. Ant.* loc. cit.). When the present custom first arose cannot be ascertained. From the description of the Chinese pilgrim Hiuen Tsiang (St. Julien, *Vie.* p. 224), who calls them Li-hi, it appears that they were still faithful to their principles in the beginning of the seventh century A.D. "The Li-hi (Nirgranthis) distinguish themselves by leaving their bodies naked and pulling out their hair. Their skin is all cracked, their feet are hard and chapped: like rotting trees that one sees near rivers."

Footnote 3: See below.

Footnote 4: In the stereotyped introductions to the sermons of Jina it is always pointed out that they are addressed to the Aryan and non-Aryan. Thus in the *Aupapâtika Sûtra* § 56. (Leumann) it runs as follows: *tesim[postvocalic] savvesim[postvocalic] âr iyamanâriyanam[postvocalic] agilâe dhammatm[postvocalic] âikkhai* "to all these, Aryans and non-Aryans, he taught the law untiringly". In accordance with this principle, conversions of people of low caste, such as gardeners, dyers, etc., are not uncommon even at the present day. Muhammadans too, regarded as Mlechcha, are still received among the Jaina communities. Some cases of the kind were communicated to me in Ah[postvocalic]madâbâd in the year 1876, as great triumphs of the Jainas. Tales of the conversion of the emperor Akbar, through the patriarch Hîravijaya (*Ind. Antiq.* Vol. XI, p. 256), and of the spread of the Digambara sect in an island Jainabhadri, in the Indian Ocean (*Ind. Ant.* Vol. VII, p. 28) and in Arabia, shew that the Jainas are familiar with the idea of the conversion of non-Indians. Hiuen Tsiang's note on the appearance of the Nirgrantha or Digambara in Kiapishi (Beal, *Si-yu-ki*, Vol. I, p. 55), points apparently to the fact that they had, in the North West at least, spread their missionary activity beyond the borders of India.

Footnote 5: Even the canonical works of the Śvetâmbara, as for example, the *Âchârâm[postvocalic] ga (Sacred Books of the East*, Vol. XXII, p. 88-186) contain directions for nuns. It seems, however, that they have never played such an important part as in Buddhism. At the present time, the few female orders among the Śvetâmbara consist entirely of virgin widows, whose husbands have died in childhood, before the beginning of their life together. It is not necessary to look upon the admission of nuns among the Śvetâmbara as an imitation of Buddhist teaching, as women were received into some of the old Brahmanical orders; see my note to *Manu*, VIII, 363, (*Sac. Bks. of the East*, Vol. XXV, p. 317). Among the Digambaras, exclusion of women was demanded from causes not far to seek. They give as their reason for it, the doctrine that women are not capable of attaining *Nirvân a*; see Peterson, *Second Report*, in *Jour. Bom. Br. R. As. Soc.* Vol. XVII, p. 84.

Footnote 6: The titles Siddha, Buddha and Mukta are certainly borrowed by both sects from the terminology of the Brâhma*n*s, which they used, even in olden times, to describe those saved during their lifetimes and used in the Śaivite doctrine to describe a consecrated one who is on the way to redemption. An Arhat, among the Brâhma*n*s, is a man distinguished for his knowledge and pious life (comp. for example Âpastamba, *Dharmasûtra.* I, 13, 13; II, 10, I.) and this idea is so near that of the Buddhists and the Jainas that it may well be looked upon as the foundation of the latter. The meaning of Tîrthakara "prophet, founder of religion", is derived from the Brâhmanic use of *tîrtha* in the sense of "doctrine". Comp. also H. Jacobi's Article on the Title of Buddha and Jina, *Sac. Books of the East*. Vol. XXII, pp. xix, xx.

Footnote 7: A Sâgara or Sâgaropamâ of years is == 100,000,000,000,000 Palya or Palyopama. A Palya is a period in which a well, of one or, according to some, a hundred *yojana*, i.e. of one or a hundred geographical square miles, stuffed full of fine hairs, can be emptied, if one hair is pulled out every hundred years: Wilson, *Select. Works*, Vol. I, p. 309; Colebrooke, *Essays*, Vol. II, p. 194. ed. Cowell.

Footnote 8: For the list of these Jinas, see below.

Footnote 9: More complete representations are to be found in Colebrooke's *Misc. Essays*. Vol. I, pp. 404, 413, with Cowell's Appendix p. 444-452; Vol. II, pp. 194, 196, 198-201; H. H. Wilson's *Select Works*, Vol. I, pp. 297-302, 305-317; J. Stevenson, *Kalpasûtra*, pp. xix-xxv; A. Barth, *Religions de l'Inde*, pp. 84-91.

Footnote 10: On the Jaina Paradise see below. Dr. Bühler seems here to have confounded the *Alôka* or Non-world, 'the space where only things without life are found', with the heaven of the Siddhas; but these are living beings who have crossed the boundary

Footnote 11: The Digambara sect, at least in southern India, do not seem to be all quite so punctiliously careful in this as the Śvetâmbara of western India.--Ed.

Footnote 12: On the five great vows see the *Âchârâm[postvocalic] ga Sûtra*, II, 15: *S.B.E.* Vol. XXII, pp. 202-210. The Sanskrit terms of the Jains are: 1. *ahim[postvocalic] sâ*, 2. *sûnrita*, 3. *asteya*, 4. *brahmâchârya*, 5. *aparigraha*; those of the Brahmanical ascetics: 1. *ahim[postvocalic] sa*, 2. *satya*, 3. *asteya*, 4. *brahmâchârya*, 5. *tyâga*.

Footnote 13: With reference to asceticism, comp. Leumann, *Aupapâtika Sûtra* § 30. The death of the wise ones by starvation is described, Weber, *Bhagavatî Sûtra*, II, 266-267; Hoernle

Upâsakadaśa Sûtra, pp. 44-62; *Âchârâm[postvocalic] ga Sûtra*, in *S.B.E.* Vol. XXII, pp. 70-73. Among the Digambara the heads of schools still, as a rule, fall victims to this fate. Even among the Śvetâmbara, cases of this kind occur, see K. Forbes, *Râs Mâlâ*, Vol. II, pp. 331-332, or 2nd ed. pp. 610-611.

Footnote 14: An example may be found in Jacobi's careful comparison of the customs of the Brâhmanic and Jaina ascetics, in the beginning of his translation of the *Âchârâm[postvocalic] ga Sûtra, S.B.E.*, Vol. XXII, pp. xxi--xxix. In relation to the death by starvation of Brahmanical hermits and Sannyâsin, see Âpastamba, *Dharmasûtra*, in S.B.E. Vol. II, pp. 154, 156, where (IT, 22, 4 and II, 23, 2) it, says of the penitents who have reached the highest grade of asceticism: "Next he shall live on water (then) on air, then on ether".

Footnote 15: The *Upâsakadaśâ Sûtra* treats of the right life of the laity, Hoernle, pp. 11-37 (Bibl. Ind.), and Hemachandra, *Yogasûtra*, Prakâsa ii and iii; Windisch, *Zeitschrift der Deutsch Morg. Ges.* Bd. XXVIII, pp. 226-246. Both scholars have pointed out in the notes to their translations, the relationship between the precepts and terms, of the Jainas and Buddhists. The Jainas have borrowed a large number of rules directly from the law books of the Brâhma*n*s. The occupations forbidden to the Jaina laity are almost all those forbidden by the Brâhmanic law to the Brâhma*n*, who in time of need lives like a Vaî śya. Hemachandra, *Yogaśâstra*, III, 98--112 and *Upâsakadaśâ Sûtra*, pp. 29-30, may be compared with Manu, X, 83-89, XI, 64 and 65, and the parallel passages quoted in the synopsis to my translation (*S.B.E.* Vol. XXV).

Footnote 16: For the Jaina ritual, see *Indian Antiquary*. Vol. XIII, pp. 191-196. The principal sacred places or Tirthas are--Sameta Śikhara in Western Bengal, where twenty of the Jinas are said to have attained Nirvâ*n*a; Śatruñjaya and Girnâr in Kâthiâwâ*d* sacred respectively to R ishabhanâtha and Neminâtha; Chandrapuri where Vâsupûjya died; and Pâwâ in Bengal at which Vardhamâna died.--Ed.

Footnote 17: The latter assertion is to be found In the *Shad darśanasamuchchaya* Vers. 45, 77-78. A creative activity is attributed to the Jinas even in the Kuhâon inscription which is dated 460-461 A.D. (*Ind. Antiq*. Vol. X, p. 126). There they are called *âdikartri* the 'original creators'. The cause of the development of a worship among the Jainas was first rightly recognised by Jacobi, *S.B.E.* Vol. XXII, p. xxi. The Jaina worship differs in one important point from that of the Buddhists. It recognised no worship of relics.

Footnote 18: A complete review of the *Am[postvocalic] ga* and the canonical works which were joined to it later, is to be found in A. Weber's fundamental treatise on the sacred writings of the Jainas in the *Indische Studien*, Bd. XVI, SS. 211-479 and Bd. XVIII, SS. 1-90. The *Âchârám[postvocalic] ga* and the *Kalpasûtra* are translated by H. Jacobi in the *S.B.E* Vol. XXII, and a part of the *Upâsakadasâ Sûtra* by R. Hoernle in the *Bibl. Ind.* In the estimates of the age of the *Am[postvocalic] ga* I follow H. Jacobi, who has throughly discussed the question *S.B.E.* Vol. XXII, pp. xxxix-xlvii.

Footnote 19: The later tradition of the Jainas gives for the death of their prophet the dates 545, 527 and 467 B.C. (see Jacobi, *Kalpasûtra* introd. pp. vii--ix and xxx). None of the sources in which these announcements appear are older than the twelfth century A.D. The latest is found in Hemachandra who died in the year 1172 A.D. The last is certainly false if the assertion, accepted by most authorities, that Buddha's death falls between the years 482 and 472 B.C. is correct. For the Buddhist tradition maintains that the last Jaina Tîrhakara died during Buddha's lifetime (see p. 34).

Footnote 20: Apart from the ill-supported supposition of Colebrooke, Stevenson and Thomas, according to which Buddha was a disloyal disciple of the founder of the Jainas, there is the view held by H. H. Wilson, A. Weber, and Lassen, and generally accepted till twenty-five years ago, that the Jainas are an old sect of the Buddhists. This was based, on the one hand, upon the resemblance of the Jaina doctrines, writings, and traditions to those of the Buddhists, on the other, on the fact that the canonical works of the Jainas show a more modern dialect than those of the Buddhists, and that authentic historical proofs of their early existence are wanting. I was myself formerly persuaded of the correctness of this view and even thought I recognised the Jainas in the Buddhist school of the Sammatîya. On a more particular examination of Jaina literature, to which I was forced on account of the collection undertaken for the English Government in the seventies, I found that the Jainas had changed their name and were always, in more ancient times, called Nirgrantha or Niga*nt*ha. The observation that the Buddhists recognise the Niga*nt*ha and relate of their head and founder, that he was a rival of Buddha's and died at Pâvâ where the last Tîrthakara is said to have attained *Nirvân a*, caused me to accept the view that the Jainas and the Buddhists sprang from the same religious movement. My supposition was confirmed by Jacobi, who reached the like view by another course, independently of mine (see *Zeitschrift der Deutsch Morg. Ges*. Bd. XXXV, S. 669. Note 1), pointing out that the last Tîrthakara in the Jaina canon bears the same name as among the Buddhists. Since the publication of our results in the *Ind. Ant*. Vol. VII, p. 143 and in Jacobi's introduction to his edition of the *Kalpasûtra,* which have been further verified by Jacobi with great penetration, views on this question have been divided. Oldenberg, Kern, Hoernle, and others have accepted this new view without hesitation, while A Weber (*Indische Studien* Bd. XVI, S. 240) and Barth (*Revue de l'Histoire des Religions*, tom. III, p. 90) keep to their former standpoint. The latter do not trust the Jaina tradition and believe it probable that the statements in the same are falsified. There are certainly great difficulties in the way of accepting such a position especially the improbability that the Buddhists should have forgotten the fact of the defection of their hated enemy. Meanwhile, this is not absolutely impossible as the oldest preserved Jaina canon had its first authentic edition only in the fifth or sixth century of our era, and as yet the proof is wanting that the Jainas, in ancient times, possessed a fixed tradition. The belief that I am able to insert this missing link in the chain of argument and the hope of removing the doubts of my two honoured friends has caused me to attempt a connected statement of the whole question although this necessitates the repetition of much that has already been said, and is in the first part almost entirely a recapitulation of the results of Jacobi's researches.

Footnote 21: The statement that Vardhamâna's father was a mighty king belongs to the manifest exaggerations. This assertion is refuted by other statements of the Jainas themselves. See Jacobi, *S.B.E.* Vol. XXII, pp. xi-xii.

Footnote 22: Dr. Bühler by a slip had here "Magadha oder Bihâr".--J. B.

Footnote 23: This is General Cunningham's identification and a probable one.--Ed.

Footnote 24: Notes on Mahâvîra's life are to be found especially in *Âchârâm[postvocalic] ga Sûtra* in *S.B.E.* Vol. XXII, pp. 84-87, 189-202; *Kalpasûtra,* ibid. pp. 217-270. The above may be compared with Jacobi's representation, ibid. pp. x-xviii. where most of the identifications of the places named are given, and *Kalpasûtra* introd. p. ii. We have to thank Dr. Hoernle for the important information that Vardhamâna's birthplace Ku*nd*apura is still called Vasukund: *Upâsakadaśâ Sûtra* p. 4. Note 3. The information on the schisms of the Jainas is collected by Lemmann in the *Indische Studien*, Bd. XVII, S. 95 ff.

Footnote 25: The *Mahâparinibbân a Sutta*, in *S.B.E.* Vol. XI, p. 106.

Footnote 26: Jacobi, *Zeitschrift der Deutsch. Morg. Ges.* Bd. XXXIV, S. 187; *Ind. Antiq.* Vol. IX, p. 159.

Footnote 27: Jacobi, *Ind. Antiq.* Vol. IX, p. 159.

Footnote 28: Jacobi, *loc. cit.*. p. 160, and Leumann, *Actes du VIième Congrès Int. des Or.* Sect. Ary. p. 505. As the Jaina accounts of the teaching of Pârśva and the existence of communities of his disciples, sound trustworthy, we may perhaps accept, with Jacobi, that they rest on a historical foundation.

Footnote 29: Jacobi *loc. cit.*. p. 159-160.

Footnote 30: See for example the account in the *Chullavagga*, in *S.B.E.* Vol. XX. p. 78-79; *Ind. Antiq.* Vol. VIII, p. 313.

Footnote 31: Spence Hardy, *Manual of Budhism*, p. 225.

Footnote 32: *S.B.E.* Vol. XVII, pp. 108-117.

Footnote 33: The passage is given in the original by Oldenberg, *Leitsch. der D. Morg. Ges.* Bd. XXXIV, S. 749. Its significance in connection with the Jaina tradition as to their schisms has been overlooked until now. It has also been unnoticed that the assertion, that Vardhamâna died during Buddha's lifetime, proves that the latest account of this occurrence given by traditions 467 B.C. is false: Later Buddhist legends (Spence Hardy, *Manual of Budhism*, pp. 266-271) treat of Nâtaputta's death in more detail. In a lengthy account they give as the cause of the same the apostacy of one of his disciples, Upâli who was converted by Buddha. After going over to Buddhism, Upâli treated his former master with scorn, and presumed to relate a parable which should prove the foolishness of those who believed in false doctrines. Thereupon the Niga*nt*ha fell into despair. He declared his alms-vessel was broken, his existence destroyed, went to Pâva, and died there. Naturally no importance is to be given to this account and its details. They are apparently the outcome of sect-hatred.

Footnote 34: According to Jacobi's supposition, *S.B.E.* Vol. XXII, p. xvi, the error was caused, by the only disciple of Vardhamâna, who outlived his master, Sudharman being an Âgniveśyâyana.

Footnote 35: See for the history of Sîha related above, Spence Hardy, *Manual of Budhism*, pp. 226, 266, and Jacobi, *Ind. Antiq.* Vol. VIII, p. 161

Footnote 36: Beal, *Si-yu-ki.* Vol. II, p. 168.

Footnote 37: Turnour, *Mahâvam[postvocalic] sa*, pp. 66-67 and p. 203, 206: *Dîpavan[g]sa* XIX 14; comp. also Kern, *Buddhismus*, Bd. I, S. 422. In the first passage in the *Mahâvam[postvocalic] sa*, three Nigha*nt*as are introduced by name, Jotiya, Giri, and Kumbha*nd*a. The translation incorrectly makes the first a Brâhma*n* and chief engineer.

Footnote 38: See Senart, *Inscriptions de Piyadasi*, tom. II, p. 82. Ed. VIII, l. 4. My translation differs from Senart's in some points especially in relation to the construction. Conf. *Epigraphia Indiea*, vol. II, pp. 272f.

Footnote 39: See *Ind. Antiquary*, vol. XX, pp. 361 ff.

Footnote 40: The meaning of these inscriptions, which were formerly believed to be Buddhist, was first made clear by Dr. Bhangvânlâl's Indrâji's careful discussion in the *Actes du VIième Congrès Internat. des Orientalistes* Sect. Ary. pp. 135-159. H; first recognised the true names of the King Khâravela and his predecessors and shewed that Khâravela and his wife were patrons of the Jainas. We have to thank him for the information that the inscription contains a date in the Maurya Era. I have thoroughly discussed his excellent article in the *Oesterreichischen Monatsschrift*, Bd. X, S. 231 ff. and have there given my reasons for differing from him on an important point, namely, the date of the beginning of the Maurya Era, which, according to his view begins with the conquest of Kalim[postvocalic] ga by Aśoka about 255 B. C. Even yet I find it impossible to accept that the expression, "in the hundred and sixty fifth year of the era of the Maurya Kings", can mean anything else than that 164 years have passed between the thirteenth year of the rule of Khâravela and the anointing of the first Maurya King Chandrugupta. Unfortunately it is impossible to fix the year of the latter occurrence, or to say more than that it took place between the years 322 and 312 B.C. The date given in Khâravela's inscription cannot therefore be more closely fixed than that it lies between 156 and 147 B.C. I now add to my former remarks--that appeals to the Arhat and Siddha appear also in Jaina inscriptions from Mathurâ and may be taken as a certain mark of the sect. Thus it is worthy of note that even in Hiuen Tsiang's time, (Beal, *Si-yu-ki*, Vol. II, p. 205) Kalinga was one of the chief seats of the Jainas.

Footnote 41: This inscription also was first made known by Dr Bhagwanlal Indiaji, *loc. cit.* p. 143.

Footnote 42: Dr. Bühler's long note (p. 48) on these inscriptions was afterwards expanded in the *Wiener Zeitschrift fur die Kunde des Morgenlandes* Bd. I, S. 165-180; Bd. II, S. 141-146. Bd. III, S. 233-240; and Bd. IV, S. 169-173. The argument of these papers is summarised in. Appendix. A, pp. 48 ff.--Ed.

Footnote 43: See Weber's and Barth's opinions quoted above in note I, p. 23.

Footnote 44: What follows is from the author's later and fuller paper in *Wiener Zeitschrift für die Kunde des Morgenlandes*, Bd. I, S. 170 f., but abridged.--Ed.

Footnote 45: The word *nirvartana* has the meaning of 'in obedience to the order', or 'in consequence of the request'. It occurs again in the Prakrit form *nivatanam[postvocalic]* below, in No. 10 (pl. xiv) and it has stood in No. 4, and at the end of l. 2 of No. 7, where the rubbing has *nirva*. It is also found in the next: *Arch. Sur. Rep.* vol. XX, pl. v, No. 6.

Footnote 46: In reading the first figure as 60, I follow Sir A. Cunningham. I have never seen the sign, in another inscription. The characters of the inscription are so archaic that this date may refer to an earlier epoch than the Indo-Skythian.

Footnote 47: *Sac. Bks. East*, vol. XXII p. 292.

Footnote 48: *S. B. E.* vol. XXII, p. 288, note 2.

Footnote 49: *Wiener Zeitshe. f. d. Kunde der Morgenl.*, Bd. II, S. 142 f.

Footnote 50: At a later date Dr. Bühler added other proofs from inscriptions of the authenticity of the Jaina tradition, in the *Vienna Oriental Journal*, vol. II, pp. 141-146; vol. III, pp. 233-240; vol. IV, pp. 169-173, 313-318; vol. V, pp. 175-180; and in *Epigraphia Indica*, vol. I pp. 371-397; vol. II, pp. 195-212, 311. The paragraphs given above are chiefly from his first paper in the *Vienna Oriental Journal* (vol. I, pp. 165-180), which appears to be an extended revision of the long footnote in the original paper on the Jainas, but it is here corrected in places from readings in his later papers.--J. B.

Footnote 51: *Epigraphia Indica*, vol. I, pp. 382, 388.

Footnote 52: For the above lists see *Wiener Zeitschi.* Bd. IV, S. 316 ff. and *Kalpasûtra* in *S. B. E.* vol. XXII, pp. 290 f.

JAINA MYTHOLOGY.

The mythology of the Jainas, whilst including many of the Hindu divinities, to which it accords very inferior positions, is altogether different in composition. It has all the appearance of a purely constructed system. The gods are classified and subdivided into orders, genera, and species; all are mortal, have their ages fixed, as well as their abodes, and are mostly distinguished by cognizances *chihnas* or *lâñchhan as*. Their Tîrthakaras, Tìrthamkaras, or perfected saints, are usually known as twenty-four belonging to the present age. But the mythology takes account also of a past and a future age or renovation of the world, and to each of these aeons are assigned twenty-four Tîrthakaras. But this is not all: in their cosmogony they lay down other continents besides Jambûdvîpa-Bharata or that which we dwell in. These are separated from Jambûdvîpa by impassable seas, but exactly like it in every respect and are called Dhâtuki-kanda and Pushkarârddha; and of each of these there are eastern, and western Bharata and Airàvata regions, whilst of Jambûdvîpa there is also a Bharata and an Airâvata region: these make the following ten regions or worlds:--

1. Jambûdvîpa-bharata-kshetra.
2. Dhâtukî-kha*nd*a pûrva-bharata.
3. Dhâtukî-kha*nd*a paśchima-bharata.
4. Pushkarârddha pûrva-bharata.
5. Pushkaravaradvîpa paśchima-bharata.
6. Jambûdvîpa airâvata-kshetra.
7. Dhâtukî-kha*nd*a pûrva-airâvata.
8. Dhâtukî-kha*nd*a paśchima-airâvata.
9. Pushkarârdhadvîpa pûrva-airâvata.
10. Puskarârddha paśchima-airâvata.

To each of these is allotted twenty four past, present and future Atîts or Jinas,--making in all 720 of this class, for which they have invented names: but they are only names. [1]

Of the Tîrthakaras of the present age or *avasarpini* in the Bharata-varsha of Jambûdvîpa, however, we are supplied with minute details:--their names, parents, stations, reputed ages, complexions, attendants, cognizances (*chihna*) or characteristics, etc. and these details are useful for the explanation of the iconography we meet with in the shrines of Jaina temples. There the images of the Tîrthakaras are placed on highly sculptured thrones and surrounded by other smaller attendant figures. In temples of the Śvetâmbara sect the images are generally of marble--white in most cases, but often black for images of the 19th, 2Oth, 22nd and 23rd Jinas. On the front of the throne or *âsana* are usually carved three small figures: at the proper right of the Jina is a male figure representing the Yaksha attendant or servant of that particular Jina; at the left end of the throne is the corresponding female--or Yakshinî, Yakshî or Śâsanadevî; whilst in a panel in the middle there is often another devî. At the base of the seat also, are placed nine very small figures representing the *navagraha* or nine planets; that is the sun, moon, five planets, and ascending and descending nodes.

In the Jaina *Purânas*, legends are given to account for the connexion of the Yakshas and Yakshîs with their respective Tîrthakaras: thus, in the case of Pârśvanâtha, we have a story of two brothers Marubhûti and Kama*t*ha, who in eight successive incarnations were always enemies, and were finally born as Pârśvanâtha and Sambaradeva respectively. A Pâsha*nd*a or unbeliever, engaged in the *panchâgni* rite, when felling a tree for his fire, against the remonstrance of Pârśvanâtha, cut in pieces two snakes that were in it; the Jina, however restored them to life by means of the *pañchamantra*. They were then re-born in Pâtâla-loka as Dhara*n*endra or Nâgendra-Yaksha and Padmâvatî-Yakshi*n*î. When Sambaradeva or Meghakumâra afterwards attacked the Arbat with a great storm, whilst he was engaged in the *Kâyotsarga* austerity--standing immovable, exposed to the weather--much in the way that Mâra attacked Śâkya Buddha at Bodh-gayâ, Dhara*n*endra's throne in Pâtâla thereupon shook, and the Nâga or Yaksha with his consort at once sped to the protection of his former benefactor. Dhara*n*endra spread his many hoods over the head of the Arhata and the Yakshm[postvocalic] î Padmâvatî held a white umbrella (*śveta chhatri*) over him for protection. Ever after they became his constant attendants, just as Śakra was to Buddha. The legend is often represented in old-sculptures, in the cave-temples at Bâdâmi, Elura, etc., and the figure of Pârśva is generally carved with the snake-hoods (*Śeshaphan i*) over him. [2]

Other legends account for the attachment of each pair of Śâsanadevatâs to their respective Jinas.

The Śvetâmbaras and Digambaras agree generally in the details respecting the different Tîrthakaras; but, from information furnished from Maisur, they seem to differ as to the names of the Yakshi*n*is attached to the several Tîrthakaras, except the first and last two; they differ also in the names of several of the Jinas of the past and the future aeons. The Digambaras enlist most of the sixteen Vidyâdevis or goddesses of knowledge among the Yakshi*n*îs, whilst the other sect include scarcely a third of them.

These Vidyâdevîs, as given by Hemachandra, are--(1) Rohi*n*î; (2) Prajñaptî; (3) Vajrasr iṅkhalâ; (4) Kuliśânkuścâ--probably the Ankuśa-Yakshî of the Śvetàmbâra fourteenth Jina; (5) Chakreśvarî; (6) Naradattâ or Purushadattâ; (7) Kâli or Kâlîkâ; (8) Mahákâlî; (9) Gaurî; (10) Gândhârî; (11) Sarvâstramahâjvâlâ; (12) Mânavî; (13) Vairo*t*yâ; (14) Achchhuptâ; (15) Mânasî; and (16) Mahâmânasikâ.

The images of the Tîrthakaras are always represented seated with their legs crossed in front--the toes of one foot resting close upon the knee of the other; and the right hand lies over the left in the lap. All are represented exactly alike except that Pârśvanâtha, the twenty-third, has the snake-hoods over him; and, with the Digambaras, Supârśva--the seventh, has also a smaller group of snake hoods. The Digambara images are all quite nude; those of the Śvetâmbaras are represented as clothed, and they decorate them with crowns and ornaments. They are distinguished from one another by their attendant *Yakshas* and *Yakshin îs* as well as by their respective *chihnas* or cognizances which are carved on the cushion of the throne.

All the Jinas are ascribed to the Ikshvâku family (*kula*)except the twentieth Munisuvrata and twenty-second Neminâtha, who were of the Harivam[postvocalic] śa race.

All received *dîkshà* or consecration at their native places; and all obtained *jńâna* or complete enlightenment at the same, except R ishabha who became a *Kevalin* at Purimatàla, Nemi at Girnâr, and Mahâvîra at the Rijupàlukà river; and twenty of them died or obtained *moksha* (deliverance in bliss) on Sameta-Śikhara or Mount Pârśvanâtha in the west of Bengal. But R ishabha, the first, died on Ash*t*âpada--supposed to be Śatruñljaya in Gujarât; Vâsupûjya died at Champâpuri in north Bengal; Neminâtha on mount Girnâr; and Mahâvîra, the last, at Pâvâpur.

Twenty-one of the Tîrthakaras are said to have attained Moksha in the Kâyotsarga (Guj. *Kâüsagga*) posture, and R ishabha, Nemi, and Mahâvira on the *padmâsana* or lotus throne.

For sake of brevity the following particulars for each Arhat are given below in serial order viz.:--

1. The *vimâna* or *vâhana* (heaven) from which he descended for incarnation.
2. Birthplace, and place of consecration or *dîkshâ.*
3. Names of father and mother.
4. Complexion.
5. Cognizance--*chihna* or *lâñchhan a.*
6. Height; and
7. Age.
8. Dîksha-vriksha or Bodhi tree.
9. Yaksha and Yakshi*n*î, or attendant spirits.
10. First Ganadhara or leading disciple, and first Âryâ or leader of the female converts.

I. R ishabhadeva, Vr ishabha, Âdinthâ or Adiśvara Bhagavân:--(I) Sarvârthasiddha; (2) Vinittanagarî in Kośalâ and Purimatâla; (3) Nâbhîrâjâ by Marudevâ; (4) golden--*varn a-*, (5)the bull,--*vr isha, balada;* (6) 500 poles or *dhanusha*; (7) 8,400,000 pûrva or great years; (8) the Va*t*a or banyan tree; (9) Gomukha and Chakreśvarî; (10) Pundarîka and Brahmî.

II. Ajitanâtha: (1) Vijayavimàna; (2) Ayodhyâ; (3) Jitaśatru by Vijayâmâtâ; (4) golden; (5) the elephant--*gaja* or *hasti*; (6) 450 poles; (7)7,200,000 pûrva years; (8) Śâla--the Shorea robusta; (9) Mahâyaksha and Ajitabalâ: with the Digambaras, the Yakshi*n*î is

Rohi*n*î-yakshî; (10) Śim[postvocalic] hasena and Phâlgu.

III. Sambhavanâtha: (1) Uvarîmagraiveka;(2) Sâvathi or Śràvasti; (3) Jitâri by Senâmâtâ; (4) golden; (5) the horse,--*aśva, ghod a*; (6) 400 poles; (7) 6,000,000 pûrva years; (8) the Prayâla--Buchanania latifolia; (9) Trimukha and Duritârî (Digambara--Prajñaptî); (10) Châru and Śyâmâ.

IV. Abhinandana: (1) Jayantavimâna; (2) Ayodhyâ; (3) Sambararâjâ by Siddhârthà; (4) golden; (5) the ape,--*plavaga, vânara* or *kapi*; (6) 350 poles; (7) 5,000,000 pûrva years; (8) the Priya*n*gu or Panicum italicum; (9) Nàyaka and Kâlîkâ, and Digambara--Yaksheśvara and Vajraśr im[postvocalic] khalâ; (10) Vajranâbha and Ajitâ.

V. Sumatinâtha: (1) Jayantavimâna; (2) Ayodhyâ; (3) Megharajâ by Mam[postvocalic] galâ; (4) golden; (5) the curlew,--*kraum[postvocalic] cha*, (Dig. *chakravakapâkshâ*--the Brâhmani or red goose); (6) 300 poles; (7) 4,000,000 pûrva years; (8) Śâla tree; (9) Tum[postvocalic] buru and Mahâkalî (Dig. Purushadattâ); (10) Charama and Kâśyapî.

VI. Padmaprabha: (1) Uvarîmagraiveka; (2) Kauśambî; (3) Śrîdhara by Susîmâ; (4) red (*rakta*); (5) a lotus bud--*padma, abja*, or *kamala*; (6) 250 poles; (7) 3,000,000 pûrva years; (8) the Chhatrâ --(Anethum sowa?); (9) Kusuma and Śyâmâ (Dig. Manovegâ or Manoguptî); (10) Pradyotana and Ratî.

VII. Supârśvanâtha: (1) Madhyamagraiveka; (2) Varâ*n*aśî; (3) Pratish*t*harâjâ by Pr ithvî; (4) golden; [3] (5) the swastika symbol; (6) 200 poles; (7) 2,000,000 pûrva years; (8) the Śirîsha or Acacia sirisha; (9) Mâtam[postvocalic] ga and Śântâ;--Digambara, Varanandi and Kâlî; (10) Vidirbha and Somâ.

VIII. Chandraprabha: (1) Vijayanta; (2) Chandrapura; (3) Mahâsenarâjâ by Lakshma*n*â; (4) white--*dhavala, śubhra*; (5) the moon--*chandrâ or śaśî*; (6) 150 poles; (7) 1,000,000 pûrva years; (8) the Nâga tree; (9) Vijaya and Bhr iku*t*î: Digambara--Śyâma or Vijaya and Jvâlâmâlinî; (10) Dinnâ and Sumanâ.

IX. Suvidhinâtha or Pushpadanta: (1) Ânatadevaloka; (2) Kâna*nd*înagarî; (3) Sugrîvarâja by Râmarâ*n*î; (4) white; (5) the Makara (Dig. the crab--*êd i*); (6) 100 poles; (7) 200,000 pûrva years; (8) the Śâlî; (9) Ajitâ and Sutârakâ: Digambara--Ajitâ and Mahâkâlî or Ajitâ; (10) Varâhaka and Vâru*n*î.

X. Śitalanâtha: (1) Achyutadevaloka; (2)Bhadrapurâ or Bhadilapura; (3) Dr ı*d*haratha-râjâ by Nandâ; (4) golden; (5) the Śrîvatsa figure: (Dig. *Śri-vriksha* the ficus religiosa); (6) 90 poles; (7) 100,000 pûrva years; (8) the Priyam[postvocalic] gu tree; (9) Brahmâ and Aśokâ (Dig. Mânavî); (10) Nandâ and Sujasâ.

XI. Śreyâm[postvocalic] śanâtha or Śreyasa: (1) Achyutadevaloka; (2) Sim[postvocalic] hapurî; (3) Vish*n*urâjâ by Vish*n*â; (4) golden; (5) the rhinoceros--*khad ga, gem[postvocalic] d â*: (Dig. Garu*d*a); (6) 80 poles; (7) 8,400,000 common years; (8) the Ta*nd*uka tree; (9) Yakshe*t* and Mânavî: Digambara--Îśvara and Gauri; (10) Kaśyapa and Dhâra*n*î.

XII. Vâsupûjya: (1) Prâ*n*atadevaloka; (2) Champâpurî; (3) Vasupûjya by Jayâ; (4) ruddy--*rakta*, Guj. *râtum[postvocalic]* ; (5) the female buffalo--*mahishî, pâdâ*; (6) 70 poles; (7) 7,200,000 common years; (8) the Pâ*t*ala or Bignonia suaveolens; (9) Kumâra and Cha*nd*â (Dig. Gândhârî); (10) Subhuma and Dhara*n*î.

XIII. Vimalanâtha: (1) Mahasâradevaloka; (2) Kampîlyapura; (3) Kr ıtavarmarâja by Śyâmâ; (4) golden; (5) a boar--*śâkara, varâha*; (6) 60 poles; (7) 6,000,000 years; (8) the Jâmbu or Eugenia jambolana; (9) Shâ*n*mukha and Viditâ (Dig. Vairô*t*î); (10) Mandara and Dharâ.

XIV. Anantanâtha or Anantajit: (1) Prâ*n*atadevaloka; (2) Ayodhyâ; (3) Sim[postvocalic] hasena by Suyaśâh[postvocalic] or Sujasâ; (4) golden; (5) a falcon--*śyena* (Dig. *bhallûka* a bear); (6) 50 poles; (7) 3,000,000 years; (8) the Aśoka or Jonesia asoka; (9) Pâtâla and Ankuśâ (Dig. Anantamatî); (10) Jasa and Padmâ.

XV. Dharmanâtha: (1) Vijayavimâna; (2) Ratnapurî; (3) Bhânurâjâ by Suvritâ; (4) golden; (5) the thunderbolt--*vajra*; (6) 45 poles; (7) 1,000,000 years; (8) Dadhîpar*n*a tree (Clitoria ternatea?); (9) Kinnara and Kandarpâ (Dig. Mânasî); (10) Arish*t*a and Ârthaśivâ.

XVI. Śântinâthâ: (1) Sarvârthasiddha; (2) Gajapura or Hastinapurî; (3) Viśvasena by Achirâ; (4) golden; (5) an antelope--*mr iga, haran a, hullĕ*, (6)40 poles; (7) 100,000 years; (8) the Nandî or Cedrela toona; (9) Garu*d*a and Nirvâ*n*î (Dig. Kimpurusha and Mahâmânasî); (10) Chakrâyuddha and Suchî.

XVII. Kunthtinâtha: (1) Sarvârthasiddha; (2) Gajapura; (3) Sûrarâjâ by Śrîrânî; (4) golden; (5) a goat--*chhâga* or *aja*; (6) 35 poles; (7) 95,000 years; (8) the Bhilaka tree; (9) Gandharva and Balâ (Dig. Vijayâ); (10) Sâmba and Dâminî.

XVIII. Aranâtha: (1) Sarvârthasiddha; (2) Gajapura; (3) Sudarśana by Devîrâ*n*î; (4) golden; (5) the Nandyâvarta diagram, (Dig. *Mina*--the zodiacal Pisces); (6) 30 poles; (7) 84,000 years; (8) Âmbâ or Mango tree; (9) Yakshe*t*a and Dha*n*â (Dig. Kendra and Ajitâ); (10) Kumbha and Rakshitâ.

XIX. Mallinâtha: (1) Jayantadevaloka; (2) Mathurâ; (3) Kumbharâjâ by Prabhâvatî; (4) blue--*nîla*; (5) a jar--*kumbham, kalaśa* or *ghat a*; (6) 25 poles; (7) 55,000 years; (8) Aśoka tree; (9) Kubera and Dhara*n*apriyâ (Dig. Aparâjitâ); (10) Abhikshaka and Bandhumatî.

XX. Munisuvrata, Suvrata or Muni: (1) Aparâjita-devaloka; (2) Râjagr iha; (3) Sumitrarâjâ by Padmâvatî; (4) black--*śyâma, asita*; (5) a tortoise--*kûrma*; (6) 20 poles; (7) 30,000 years; (8) the Champaka, Michelia champaka; (9) Varu*n*a and Naradattâ, (Dig. Bahurûpi*n*î); (10) Malli and Pushpavatî.

XXI. Naminâtha, Nimi or Nimeśvara: (1) Prâ*n*atadevaloka; (2) Mathurâ; (3) Vijayarâjâ by Viprârâ*n*î; (4) yellow; (5) the blue water-lily--*nîlotpala*, with the Digambaras, sometimes the Aśoka tree; (6) 15 poles; (7) 10,000 years; (8) the Bakula or Mimusops elengi; (9) Bhr iku*t*i and Gandhârî, (Dig. Châmu*nd*î); (10) Śubha and Anilâ.

XXII. Neminâtha or Arish*t*anemi: (1) Aparâjita; (2) Sauripura (Prákrit--Soriyapura) and Ujjinta or Mount Girnâr; (3) Samudravijaya by Śivâdevi; (4) black--*śyâma*; (5) a conch,--*śam[postvocalic] kha*; (6) 10 poles; (7) 1000 years; (8) the Ve*t*asa; (9) Gomedha and Ambikâ: with the Digambaras, Sarvâh*n*a and Kûshmâ*nd*inî; (10) Varadatta and Yakshadinnâ.

XXIII. Pârśvanâtha: (1) Prâ*n*atadevaloka; (2) Vârâ*n*asî and Sameta-Śikhara; (3) Aśvasenarâja by Vâmâdevî; (4) blue--*nîla*; (5) a serpent--*sarpa*; (6) 9 hands; (7) 100 years; (8) the Dhâtakî or Grislea tomentosa; (9) Pârśvayaksha or Dhara*n*endra and Padmâvatî; (10) Âryadinna and Pushpachû*d*â.

XXIV. Śri-Mahâvîra, Vardhamâna or Vîra, the Śrama*n*a: (1) Prâ*n* atadevaloka; (2) Ku*nd*agrâma or Chitrakû*t*a, and R ijupâlukâ; (3) Siddhârtharâja, Śreyânśa or Yaśasvin by Triśalâ Vidchadinnâ or Priyakâri*n*î; (4) yellow; (5) a lion--*keśarî-simha*; (6) 7 hands or cubits; (7) 72 years; (8) the *śala* or teak tree; (9) Mâtam[postvocalic] ga and Siddhâyikâ; (10) Indrabhûti and Chandrabâlâ.

The Tirthakuras may be regarded as the *dii majores* of the Jainas, [4] though, having become Siddhas, emancipated from all concern, they can have no interest in mundane affairs. They and such beings as are supposed to have reached perfection are divided into fifteen species:

1. Tîrthakarasiddhas;
2. Atîrthakarasiddhas;
3. Tîrthasiddhas;
4. Svalim[postvocalic] gasiddas;
5. Anyalim[postvocalic] gasiddhas;
6. Strilim[postvocalic] gasiddhas;
7. Purushalim[postvocalic] gasiddhas;
8. Napum[postvocalic] sakalim[postvocalic] gasiddhas;
9. Gr ihalim[postvocalic] gasiddhas;
10. Tîrthavyavachchhedasiddhas;
11. Pratyekabuddhasiddhas;
12. Svayambuddhasiddhas;
13. Ekasiddas;
14. Anekasiddhas;
15. Buddhabodhietasiddllas.

[5]

But the gods are divided into four classes, and each class into several orders: the four classes are:--

I. Bhavanâdhipatis, Bhavanavâsins or Bhaumeyikas, of which there are ten orders, viz.--

1. Asurakumâras;
2. Nâgakumâras;
3. Ta*d*itkumâras or Vidyutkumâras;
4. Suvar*n*a- or Suparnaka-kumâras;
5. Agnikumâras;
6. Dvîpakumâras (Dîvakumâras);
7. Udadhikumâras;
8. Dikkumâras;
9. Pavana- or Vâta-kumâras;
10. Gha*n*ika- or Sanitakumâras.

II. Vyantaras or Vâ*n*amantaras, who live in woods are of eight classes:--

1. Piśâchas;
2. Bhûtas;
3. Yakshas;
4. Râkshasas;
5. Kimnaras;
6. Kimpurushas;
7. Mahoragas;
8. Gandharvas.

III. The Jyotishkas are the inhabitants of;

1. Chandras or the moons;
2. Sûryas or the suns;
3. Grahas or the planets;
4. Nakshatras or the constellations;
5. Târâs or the hosts of stars.

And IV. The Vaimânika gods are of two orders: (1) the Kalpabhavas, who are born in the heavenly Kalpas; and (2) the Kalpâtîtas, born in the regions above the Kalpas.

(1) The Kalpabhavas again are subdivided into twelve genera who live in the Kalpas after which they are named; viz,--

1. Saudharma;
2. Îśâna;
3. Sanatkumâra;
4. Mâhendra;
5. Brahmaloka;

6. Lântaka;
7. Śukra or Mahâśukla;
8. Sahasrâra;
9. Ânata (Â*n*aya);
10. Prâ*n*ata (Pâ*n*aya);
11. Âra*n*a;
12. Achyuta.

(2) The Kalpâtîtas are subdivided into-- (a) the Graiveyakas, living on the upper part of the universe; and (b) the Anuttaras or those above whom there are no others.

(a) The Graiveyakas are of nine species, viz.--

1. Sudarsa*n*as;
2. Supratipandhas;
3. Ma*n*oramas;
4. Sarvabhadras;
5. Suviśâlas;
6. Soma*n*asas;
7. Sumam[postvocalic] kasas;
8. Prîyam[postvocalic] karas;
9. Âdityas or Nandikaras.

(b) the Anuttara gods are of five orders: viz.--

1. Vijayas;
2. Vaijayantas;
3. Jayantas;
4. Aparâjitas; and
5. Sarvârthasiddhas.

[6]

These Anuttara gods inhabit the highest heavens where they live for varying lengths of time as the heavens ascend; and in the fifth or highest--the great Vimâna called Sarvârthasiddha--they all live thirty-three Sâgaropamas or periods of unimagiable duration. Still all the gods are mortal or belong to the *sam[postvocalic] sâra*.

Above these is the paradise of the Siddhas or perfected souls, and the *Uttarâdhyana Sûtra* gives the following details of this realm of the perfected, or the paradise of the Jainas:--

[7]

"The perfected souls are those of women, men, hermaphrodites, of orthodox, heterodox, and householders. Perfection is reached by people of the greatest, smallest and middle size; [8] on high places, underground, on the surface of the earth, in the ocean, and in waters (of rivers, etc.).

"Ten hermaphrodites reach perfection at the same time, twenty women, one hundred and eight men; four householders, ten heterodox, and one hundred and eight orthodox monks.

"Two individuals of the greatest size reach perfection (simultaneously), four of the smallest size, and one hundred and eight of the middle size. Four individuals reach perfection (simultaneously) on high places, two in the ocean, three in water, twenty underground; and where do they go on reaching perfection? Perfected souls are debarred from the non-world (Aloka); they reside on the top of the world; they leave their bodies here (below) and go there, on reaching perfection.

"Twelve *yojanas* above the (Vimâna) Sarvârtha is the place called Îshatpragbhâra, which has the form of an umbrella; (there the perfected souls go). It is forty-five hundred thousand *yojanas* long, and as many broad, and it is somewhat more than three times as many in circumference. Its thickness is eight *yojanas*, it is greatest in the middle, and decreases towards the margin, till it is thinner than the wing of a fly. This place, by nature pure, consisting of white gold, resembles in form an open umbrella, as has been said by the best of Jinas.

"(Above it) is a pure blessed place (called Śîtâ), which is white like a conch-shell, the *anka*-stone, and Kunda-flowers; [9] a *yojana* thence is the end of the world. The perfected souls penetrate the sixth part of the uppermost *krośa* of the (above-mentioned) *yojana*. There, at the top of the world reside the blessed perfected souls, rid of all transmigration, and arrived at the excellent state of perfection. The dimension of a perfected soul is two-thirds of the height which the individual had in his last existence.

"The perfected souls considered singly--*êgattên a* (as individuals)--have a beginning but no end, considered collectively--*puhuttên a* (as a class)--they have neither a beginning nor an end. They have no (visible) form, they consist of life throughout, they are developed into knowledge and faith, they have crossed the boundary of the Sam[postvocalic] sâra, and reached the excellent state of perfection."

Like both the Brâhma*n*s and Buddhists, the Jainas have a series of hells--Nârakas, numbering even which they name--

1. Ratnaprabhâ;
2. Śarkarâprabhâ;
3. Vâlukâprabhâ;
4. Pam[postvocalic] kaprabhâ;
5. Dhûmaprabhâ;
6. Tamaprabhâ;
7. Tamatamaprabhâ.

[10]

Those who inhabit the seventh hell have a stature of 500 poles, and in each above that they are half the height of the one below it.

Everything in the system as to stature of gods and living beings, their ages and periods of transmigration is reduced to artificial numbers.

The Jaina Gachhas.

About the middle of the tenth century there flourished a Jaina high priest named Uddyotana, with whose pupils the eighty four gachhas originated. This number is still spoken of by the Jainas, but the lists that have been hitherto published are very discordant. The following was obtained from a member of the sect as being their recognised list,--and allowing for differences of spelling, nearly every name may be recognised in those previously published by Mr. H. G. Briggs or Colonel Miles.

The Eighty four Gachchhas of the Jainas. [11]

1. ? *†
2. Osvâla*†
3. Âm[postvocalic] chala*
4. Jirâvalâ*†
5. Kha*d*atara or Kharatara
6. Lonkâ or Richmati*†
7. Tapâ*†
8. Gam[postvocalic] geśvara*†
9. Kora*nt*avâla†
10. Ânandapura†
11. Bharavalî
12. U*d*havîyâ*†
13. Gudâvâ*†
14. Dekâüpâ or Dekâwâ*†
15. Bh nmâlâ†

22. Vîka*d*îyâ*†
23. Muñjhîyâ*†
24. Chitro*d*â†
25. Sâchorâ*†
26. Jacha*nd*îyâ†
27. Sîdhâlavâ*†
28. Mîyâ*nn*îyâ
29. Âgamîyâ†
30. Maladhârî*†
31. Bhâvarîyâ†
32. Palîvâla*†
33. Nâgadîgeśvara†
34. Dharmaghosha†
35. Nâgapurâ*†
36. Uchatavâla†
37. Nâ*nn*âvâla*†
38. Sâ*d*erâ*†
39. Ma*nd*ovarâ*†
40. Śurâ*n*î*†
41.

43. Sopârîyâ*†
44. Mâ*nd*alîyâ*†
45. Kochhîpanâ*†
46. Jâgam[postvocalic] na*†
47. Lâparavâla*†
48. Vosara*d*â*†
49. Düîvam[postvocalic] danîyâ*†
50. Chitrâvâla*†
51. Vega*d*â
52. Vâpa*d*â
53. Vîjaharâ, Vîjharâ*†
54. Kâüpurî†
55. Kâchala
56. Ham[postvocalic] dalîyâ†
57. Mahukarâ†
58. Putaliyâ*†
59.

16. Mahud*i*yâ*†	Kham[postvocalic]	Kam[postvocalic]
17. Gachhapâla*†	bhâvatî*†	narîsey†
18. Goshavâla†	42.	60. Revar*d*ıyâ*†
19.	Pâëcham[postvocalic]	61. Dhandhukâ†
Magatragagadâ†	da	62.
20. Vr ihmânîyâ†		Tham[postvocalic]
21. Tâlârâ*†		bhanîpa*n*â*
		63.
		Pam[postvocalic]
		chîvâla†

Sketch of Jaina Mythology

FOOTNOTES

Footnote 1: See *Ratnasâgara*, bh. II, pp. 696--705.
Footnote 2: *Cave Temples*, pp. 491, 496; *Arch. Sur. Westn. India*, vol. I, p. 25 and pl. xxxvii; vol. V, p. 49; *Transactions, R. As. Soc.*, vol. I, p. 435. At Rânpur in Godwâr, in the temple of Rishabhanâtha is a finely carved slab representing Pârśvanâtha in the Kâyotsarga position, attended by snake divinities,--*Archit. and Scenery in Gujarât and Râjputâna*, p. 21. The story has variants: conf. *Ind. Ant.* vol. XXX, p. 302.
Footnote 3: The Digambara describe the colours of the seventh and twenty-first Jinas as *marakada* or emerald coloured.
Footnote 4: For an account of the ritual of the Svetâmbara sect of Jainas, see my account in the *Indian Antiquary*, vol. XIII, pp. 191-196.
Footnote 5: *Jour. Asiat.* IXme Ser. tom. XIX, p. 260.
Footnote 6: Conf. *Ratnasâgara*, bh. II, pp. 616, 617; *Jour. Asiat.* IXme Ser. tome XIX, p. 259; *Sac. Bks. E.*

vol. XLV, p. 226 f. See also *Rev. de l'Histoire des Relig.* tom. XLVII, pp. 34-50, which has appeared since the above was written, for "La doctrine des êtres vivants dans la Religion Jaina".

Footnote 7: See *ante*, p. 11, note 10; The following extract is from *Sac. Books of the East*, vol. XLV, pp. 211-213.

Footnote 8: The greatest size--*ogâhan â*--of men is 500 dhanush or 2000 cubits, the smallest is one cubit.

Footnote 9: The gourd Lagenaria vulgaris.

Footnote 10: *Ratnasâgara*, bh. II, p. 607; *Jour. As.* u.s. p. 263.

Footnote 11: Those names marked * are found in Col. Miles's list *Tr. R. A. S.* vol. III, pp. 358 f. 363, 365, 370. Those marked † are included in H. G. Brigg's list,--*Cities of Gujarashtra*, p. 339.

Note to the HTML edition: This document duplicates the diacritical marks of the original using HTML unicode combining character entities. Not all browsers and operating systems support them. The chart below shows how these unusual characters are displayed in your browser.

Diacritical marks used in this document					
Â	circumflex over A	ĭ	breve over i	ṇ	dot under n
â	circumflex over a	ī	macron over i	ñ	tilde over n
à	grave over a	Î	circumflex over I	ô	circumflex over o
á	acute over a	î	circumflex over i	ṛ	dot under r
ḍ	dot under d	í	acute over i	Ṛ	dot under R
ĕ	breve over e	ì	grave over i	Ś	acute over S
è	grave over e	Ṁ	dot over M	ś	acute over s

ê	circumflex over e	ṁ	dot over m	Ṭ	dot under T
ë	umlaut over e	ṃ	dot under m	ṭ	dot under t
ḥ	dot under h	n̄	macron over n	Ü	umlaut over U
î	circumflex over i	ń	acute over n	ü	umlaut over u
i̐	chandrabindu over i	ṅ	dot over n	û	circumflex over u

ON THE INDIAN SECT OF THE JAINAS

BY
JOHANN GEORG BÜHLER C.I.E., LLD., PH.D.
Member of the Imperial Academy of Sciences, Vienna.

TRANSLATED FROM THE GERMAN.

EDITED
with an
OUTLINE of JAINA MYTHOLOGY

BY
JAS. BURGESS, C.I.E., LL.D., F.R.S.E.

1903.

CONTENTS.

PREFACE.

The late Dr. Georg Bühler's essay *Ueber die Indische Secte der Jaina*, read at the anniversary meeting of the Imperial Academy of Sciences of Vienna on the 26th May 1887, has been for some time out of print in the separate form. Its value as a succinct account of the Śrâvaka sect, by a scholar conversant with them and their religious literature is well known to European scholars; but to nearly all educated natives of India works published in German and other continental languages are practically sealed books, and thus the fresh information which they are well able to contribute is not elicited. It is hoped that the translation of this small work may meet with their acceptance and that of Europeans in India and elsewhere to whom the original is either unknown or who do not find a foreign language so easy to read as their own.

The translation has been prepared under my supervision, and with a few short footnotes. Professor Bühler's long note on the authenticity of the Jaina tradition I have transferred to an appendix (p. 48) incorporating with it a summary of what he subsequently expanded in proof of his thesis.

To Colebrooke's account of the Tirthaṅkaras reverenced by the Jainas, but little has been added since its publication in the ninth volume of the *Asiatic Researches*; and as these are the centre of their worship, always represented in their temples, and surrounded by attendant figures,--I have ventured to add a somewhat fuller account of them and a summary of the general mythology of the sect, which may be useful to the archaeologist and the student of their iconography.

Edinburgh, April 1903. **J. BURGESS.**

THE INDIAN SECT OF THE JAINAS.

The *Jaina* sect is a religious society of modern India, at variance to Brahmanism, and possesses undoubted claims on the interest of all friends of Indian history. This claim is based partly on the peculiarities of their doctrines and customs, which present several resemblances to those of Buddhism, but, above all, on the fact that it was founded in the same period as the latter.

Larger and smaller communities of *Jainas* or *Arhata*,--that is followers of the prophet, who is generally called simply the *Jina*--'the conqueror of the world',--or the *Arhat*--'the holy one',--are to be found in almost every important Indian town, particularly among the merchant class. In some provinces of the West and North-west, in Gujarât, Râjputâna, and the Panjâb, as also in the Dravidian districts in the south,--especially in Kanara,--they are numerous; and, owing to the influence of their wealth, they take a prominent place. They do not, however, present a compact mass, but are divided into two rival branches--the *Digambara* and *Śvetâmbara*[1] --each of which is split up into several subdivisions. The Digambara, that is, "those whose robe is the atmosphere," owe their name to the circumstance that they regard absolute nudity as the indispensable sign of holiness, [2] --though the advance of civilization has compelled them to depart from the practice of their theory. The Śvetâmbara, that is, "they who are clothed in white"--do not claim this doctrine, but hold it as possible that the holy ones, who clothe themselves, may also attain the highest goal. They allow, however, that the founder of the Jaina religion and his first disciples disdained to wear clothes. They are divided, not only by this quarrel, but also by differences about dogmas and by a different literature. The separation must therefore be of old standing. Tradition, too, upholds this--though the dates given do not coincide. From inscriptions it is certain that the split occurred before the first century of our era. [3] Their opposing opinions are manifested in the fact that they do not allow each other the right of intermarriage or of eating at the same table,--the two chief marks of social equality. In spite of the age of the schism, and the enmity that divides the two branches, they are at one as regards the arrangement of their communities, doctrine, discipline, and cult,--at least in the more important points; and, thus, one can always speak of the Jaina religion as a whole.

The characteristic feature of this religion is its claim to universality, which it holds in common with Buddhism, and in opposition to Brahmanism. It also declares its object to be to lead all men to salvation, and to open its arms--not only to the noble Aryan, but also to the low-born Śûdra and even to the alien, deeply despised in India, the Mlechcha. [4] As their doctrine, like Buddha's, is originally a philosophical ethical system intended for ascetics, the disciples, like the Buddhists, are, divided into ecclesiastics and laity. At the head stands an order of ascetics, originally Nirgrantha "they, who are freed from all bands," now usually called Yatis--"Ascetics", or Sâdhus--"Holy", which, among the Śvetâmbara also admits women, [5] and under them the general community of the Upâsaka "the Worshippers", or the Śrâvaka, "the hearers".

The ascetics alone are able to penetrate into the truths which Jina teaches, to follow his rules and to attain to the highest reward which he promises. The laity, however, who do not dedicate themselves to the search after truth, and cannot renounce the life of the world, still find a refuge in Jainism. It is allowed to them as hearers to share its principles, and to undertake duties, which are a faint copy of the demands made on the ascetics. Their reward is naturally less. He who remains in the world cannot reach the highest goal, but he can still tread the way which leads to it. Like all religions of the Hindûs founded on philosophical speculation, Jainism sees this highest goal in *Nirvâna* or *Moksha*, the setting free of the individual from the *Saṁsâra*,--the revolution of birth and death. The means of reaching it are to it, as to Buddhism, the three Jewels--the right Faith, the right Knowledge, and the right Walk. By the right Faith it understands the full surrender of himself to the teacher, the Jina, the firm conviction that he alone has found the way of salvation, and only with him is protection and refuge to be found. Ask who Jina is, and the Jaina will give exactly the same answer as the Buddhist with respect to Buddha. He is originally an erring man, bound with the bonds of the world, who,--not by the help of a teacher, nor by the revelation of the Vedas--which, he declares, are corrupt--but by his own power, has attained to omniscience and freedom, and out of pity for suffering mankind preaches and declares the way of salvation, which he has found. Because he has conquered the world and the enemies in the human heart, he is called Jina "the Victor", Mahâvîra, "the great hero"; because he possesses the highest knowledge, he is called Sarvajña or Kevalin, the "omniscient", Buddha, the "enlightened"; because he has freed himself from the world he receives the names of Mukta "the delivered one", Siddha and Tathâgata, "the perfected", Arhat "the holy one"; and as the proclaimer of the doctrine, he is the Tîrthakara "the finder of the ford", through the ocean of the *Saṁsâra*. In these epithets, applied to the founder of their doctrine, the Jainas agree almost entirely with the Buddhists, as the likeness of his character to that of Buddha would lead us to expect. They prefer, however, to use the names Jina and Arhat, while the Buddhists prefer to speak of Buddha as Tathâgata or Sugata. The title Tîrthakara is peculiar to the Jainas. Among the Buddhists it is a designation for false teachers. [6]

The Jaina says further, however, that there was more than one Jina. Four and twenty have, at long intervals, appeared and have again and again restored to their original purity the doctrines darkened by evil influences. They all spring from noble, warlike tribes. Only in such, not among the low Brâhmaṇs, can a Jina see the light of the world. The first Jina Ṛishabha,--more than 100 billion oceans of years ago,--periods of unimaginable length, [7] --was born as the son of a king of Ayodhyâ and lived eight million four hundred thousand years. The intervals between his successors and the durations of their lives became shorter and shorter. Between the twenty third, Pârśva and the twenty fourth Vardhamâna, were only 250 years, and the age of the latter is given as only seventy-two years. He appeared, according to some, in the last half of the sixth century, according to others in the first half of the fifth century B.C. He is of course the true, historical prophet of the Jainas and it is in his doctrine, that the Jainas should believe. The dating back of the origin of the Jaina religion again, agrees with the pretensions of the Buddhists, who recognise twenty-five

Buddhas who taught the same system one after the other. Even with Brahmanism, it seems to be in some distant manner connected, for the latter teaches in its cosmogony, the successive appearance of Demiurges, and wise men--the fourteen Manus, who, at various periods helped to complete the work of creation and proclaimed the Brahmanical law. These Brahmanical ideas may possibly have given rise to the doctrines of the twenty-five Buddhas and twenty-four Jinas, [8] which, certainly, are later additions in both systems.

The undoubted and absolutely correct comprehension of the nine truths which the Jina gives expression to, or of the philosophical system which the Jina taught, represents the second Jewel--the true Knowledge. Its principal features are shortly as follows. [9]

The world (by which we are to understand, not only the visible, but also imaginary continents depicted with the most extravagant fancy, heavens and hells of the Brahmanical Cosmology, extended by new discoveries) is uncreated. It exists, without ruler, only by the power of its elements, and is everlasting. The elements of the world are six substances--souls, *Dharma* or moral merit, *Adharma* or sin, space, time, particles of matter. From the union of the latter spring four elements--earth, fire, water, wind--and further, bodies and all other appearances of the world of sense and of the supernatural worlds. The forms of the appearances are mostly unchangeable. Only the bodies of men and their age increase or decrease in consequence of the greater or less influence of sin or merit, during immeasurably long periods,--the *Avasarpiṇi* and the *Utsarpiṇi*. Souls are, each by itself, independent, real existences whose foundation is pure intelligence, and who possess an impulse to action. In the world they are always chained to bodies. The reason of this confinement is that they give themselves up to the stress of activity, to passions, to influences of the senses and objects of the mind, or attach themselves to a false belief. The deeds which they perform in the bodies are *Karman*, merit and sin. This drives them--when one body has passed away, according to the conditions of its existence--into another, whose quality depends on the character of the *Karman*, and will be determined especially by the last thoughts springing from it before death. Virtue leads to the heavens of the gods or to birth among men in pure and noble races. Sin consigns the souls to the lower regions, in the bodies of animals, in plants, even into masses of lifeless matter. For--according to the Jaina doctrine--souls exist not only in organic structures, but also in apparently dead masses, in stones, in lumps of earth, in drops of water, in fire and in wind. Through union with bodies the nature of the soul is affected. In the mass of matter the light of its intelligence is completely concealed; it loses consciousness, is immovable, and large or small, according to the dimensions of its abode. In organic structures it is always conscious; it depends however, on the nature of the same, whether it is movable or immovable and possessed of five, four, three, two, or one organ of sense.

The bondage of souls, if they inhabit a human body, can be abolished by the suppression of the causes which lead to their confinement and by the destruction of the *Karman*. The suppression of the causes is accomplished by overcoming the inclination to be active and the passions, by the control of the senses, and by steadfastly holding to the right faith. In this way will be hindered the addition of new *Karman*, new merit or new guilt. The destruction of *Karman* remaining from previous existences can be brought about either spontaneously by the exhaustion of the supply or by asceticism. In the latter case the final state is the attainment to a knowledge which penetrates the universe, to *Kevala, Jñâna* and *Nirvâṇa* or *Moksha*: full deliverance from all bonds. These goals may be reached even while the soul is still in its body. If however the body is destroyed then the soul wanders into the "No-World" *(alôka)* as the Jain says, i.e. into the heaven of Jina 'the delivered', lying outside the world. [10] There it continues eternally in its pure intellectual nature. Its condition is that of perfect rest which nothing disturbs. These fundamental ideas are carried out in the particulars with a subtilness and fantasy unexampled, even in subtile and fantastic India, in a scholarly style, and defended by the *syâdvâda*--the doctrine of "It may be so",--a mode of reasoning which makes it possible to assert and deny the existence of one and the same thing. If this be compared with the other Indian systems, it stands nearer the Brâhmaṇ than the Buddhist, with which it has the acceptance in common of only four, not five elements. Jainism touches all the Brâhmaṇ religions and Buddhism in its cosmology and ideas of periods, and it agrees entirely with regard to the doctrines of *Karman*, of the bondage, and the deliverance of souls. Atheism, the view that the world was not created, is common to it with Buddhism and the Sâṅkhya philosophy. Its psychology approaches that of the latter in that both believe in the existence of innumerable independent souls. But the doctrine of the activity of souls and their distribution into masses of matter is in accordance with the Vedânta, according to which the principle of the soul penetrates every thing existing. In the further development of the soul doctrine, the conceptions 'individual soul' and 'living being' to which the Jaina and the Brâhmaṇ give the same name,--*jîva*, seem to become confounded. The Jaina idea of space and time as real substances is also found in the Vaiśeshika system. In placing *Dharma* and *Adharma* among substances Jainism stands alone.

The third jewel, the right Walk which the Jaina ethics contains, has its kernel in the five great oaths which the Jaina ascetic takes on his entrance into the order. He promises, just as the Brâhmaṇ penitent, and almost in the same words, not to hurt, not to speak untruth, to appropriate nothing to himself without permission, to preserve chastity, and to practice self-sacrifice. The contents of these simple rules become most extraordinarily extended on the part of the Jainas by the insertion of five clauses, in each of which are three separate active instruments of sin, in special relation to thoughts, words, and deeds. Thus, concerning the oath not to hurt, on which the Jaina lays the greatest emphasis: it includes not only the intentional killing or hurting of living beings, plants, or the souls existing in dead matter, it requires also the utmost carefulness in the whole manner of life, in all movements, a watchfulness over all functions of the body by which anything living might be hurt. [11] It demands finally strict watch over the heart and tongue, and the avoidance of all thoughts and words which might lead to dispute and quarrel and thereby to harm. In like manner the rule of sacrifice means not only that the ascetic has no house or possessions, it teaches also that a complete unconcern toward agreeable and disagreeable impressions is necessary, as also the sacrifice of every attachment to anything living or dead. [12]

Beside the conscientious observance of these rules, Tapas--Asceticism, is most important for the right walk of those, who strive to attain *Nirvâṇa.* Asceticism is inward as well as outward. The former is concerned with self-discipline, the cleansing and purifying of the mind. It embraces repentance of sin, confession of the same to the teacher, and penance done for it, humility before teachers and all virtuous ones, and the service of the same, the study and teaching of the faith or holy writing, pious meditations on the misery of the world, the impurity of the body, etc. and lastly, the stripping off of every thing pertaining to the world. On the other hand, under the head of exterior Asceticism, the Jaina understands temperance, begging, giving up all savoury food, different kinds of self-mortification such as sitting in unnatural and wearying positions, hindering the action of the organs, especially by fasts, which, under certain circumstances may be continued to starvation. Voluntary death by the withdrawal of nourishment is, according to the strict doctrine of the Digambara, necessary for all ascetics, who have reached the highest step of knowledge. The Kevalin, they say, eats no longer. The milder Śvetâmbara do not demand this absolutely, but regard it, as a sure entrance to *Nirvâṇa.* In order, however, that this death may bear its fruits, the ascetic must keep closely to the directions for it, otherwise he merely lengthens the number of rebirths. [13]

From these general rules follow numerous special ones, regarding the life of the disciple of Jina. The duty of sacrifice forces him, on entrance into the order, to give up his possessions and wander homeless in strange lands, alms-vessel in hand, and, if no other duty interferes, never to stay longer than one night in the same place. The rule of wounding nothing means that he must carry three articles with him, a straining cloth, for his drinking water, a broom, and a veil before his mouth, in order to avoid killing insects. It also commands him to avoid all cleansing and washing, and to rest in the four months of the rainy season, in which animal and plant life displays itself most abundantly. In order to practice asceticism, it is the rule to make this time of rest a period of strictest fasts, most diligent study of the holy writings, and deepest meditation. This duty also necessitates the ascetic to pluck out in the most painful manner his hair which, according to oriental custom, he must do away with at his consecration--a peculiar custom of the Jainas, which is not found among other penitents of India.

Like the five great vows, most of the special directions for the discipline of the Jain ascetic are copies, and often exaggerated copies, of the Brâhmanic rules for penitents. The outward marks of the order closely resemble those of the Sannyâsin. The life of wandering during eight months and the rest during the rainy season agree exactly; and in many other points, for example in the use of confession, they agree with the Buddhists. They agree with Brâhmaṇs alone in ascetic self-torture, which Buddhism rejects; and specially characteristic is the fact that ancient Brâhmanism recommends starvation to its penitents as beneficial. [14]

The doctrine of the right way for the Jaina laity differs from that for the ascetics. In place of the five great vows appear mere echoes. He vows to avoid only serious injury to living beings, i.e. men and animals; only the grosser forms of untruth--direct lies; only the most flagrant forms of taking, what is not given, that is, theft and robbery. In place of the oath of chastity there is that of conjugal fidelity. In place of that of self-denial, the promise is not greedily to accumulate possessions and to be contented. To these copies are added seven other vows, the miscellaneous contents of which correspond to the special directions for the discipline of ascetics. Their object is, partly to bring the outward life of the laity into accordance with the Jaina teaching, especially with regard to the protection of living creatures from harm, and partly to point the heart to the highest goal. Some contain prohibitions against certain drinks, such as spirits; or meats, such as flesh, fresh butter, honey, which cannot be enjoyed without breaking the vow of preservation of animal life. Others limit the choice of businesses which the laity may enter; for example, agriculture is forbidden, as it involves the tearing up of the ground and the death of many animals, as Brâhmanism also holds. Others have to do with mercy and charitableness, with the preserving of inward peace, or with the necessity of neither clinging too much to life and its joys nor longing for death as the end of suffering. To the laity, however, voluntary starvation is also recommended as meritorious. These directions (as might be expected from the likeness of the circumstances) resemble in many points the Buddhist directions for the laity, and indeed are often identical with regard to the language used. Much is however specially in accordance with Brâhmanic doctrines. [15] In practical life Jainism makes of its laity earnest men who exhibit a stronger trait of resignation than other Indians and excel in an exceptional willingness to sacrifice anything for their religion. It makes them also fanatics for the protection of animal life. Wherever they gain influence, there is an end of bloody sacrifices and of slaughtering and killing the larger animals.

The union of the laity with the order of ascetics has, naturally, exercised a powerful reaction on the former and its development, as well as on its teaching, and is followed by similar results in Jainism and Buddhism. Then, as regards the changes in the teaching, it is no doubt to be ascribed to the influence of the laity that the atheistic Jaina system, as well as the Buddhist, has been endowed with a cult. The ascetic, in his striving for *Nirvâṇa*, endeavours to suppress the natural desire of man to worship higher powers. In the worldly hearer, who does not strive after this goal exclusively, this could not succeed. Since the doctrine gave no other support, the religious feeling of the laity clung to the founder of it: Jina, and with him his mythical predecessors, became gods. Monuments and temples ornamented with their statues were built, especially at those places, where the prophets, according to legends, had reached their goal. To this is added a kind of worship, consisting of offerings of flowers and incense to Jina, of adoration by songs of praise in celebration of their entrance into *Nirvâṇa*, of which the Jaina makes a great festival by solemn processions and pilgrimages to the places where it has been attained. [16] This influence of the laity has become, in course of time, of great importance to Indian art, and India is indebted to it for a number of its most beautiful architectural monuments, such as the splendid temples of Âbu, Girnâr and Śatruñjaya in Gujarât. It has also brought about a change in the mind of the ascetics. In many of their hymns in honour of Jina, they appeal to him with as much fervour as the Brâhmaṇ to his gods; and there are often expressions in them, contrary, to the original teaching, ascribing to Jina a creative power. Indeed a Jaina description of the six principal systems goes so far as to number Jainism--as also Buddhism--among the theistic religions. [17]

But in other respects also the admission of the laity has produced decisive changes in the life of the clergy. In the education of worldly communities, the ascetic--whose rules of indifference toward all and every thing, make him a being concentrated entirely upon himself and his goal--is united again to humanity and its interests. The duty of educating the layman and watching over his life, must of necessity change the wandering penitents into settled monks--who dedicate themselves to the care of souls, missionary activity, and the acquisition of knowledge, and who only now and again fulfil the duty of changing their place of residence. The needs of the lay communities required the continual presence of teachers. Even should these desire to change from time to time, it was yet necessary to provide a shelter for them. Thus the Upâśraya or places of refuge, the Jaina monasteries came into existence, which exactly correspond to the Buddhist Sanghârâma. With the monasteries and the fixed residence in them appeared a fixed membership of the order, which, on account of the Jaina principle of unconditional obedience toward the teacher, proved to be much stricter than in Buddhism. On the development of the order and the leisure of monastic life, there followed further, the commencement of a literary and scientific activity. The oldest attempt, in this respect, limited itself to bringing their doctrine into fixed forms. Their results were, besides other lost works, the so-called *Aṅga*,--the members of the body of the law, which was perhaps originally produced in the third century B.C. Of the *Aṅga* eleven are no doubt preserved among the Śvetâmbaras from a late edition of the fifth or sixth century A.D. These works are not written in Sanskrit, but in a popular Prâkrit dialect: for the Jina, like Buddha, used the language of the people when teaching. They contain partly legends about the prophet and his activity as a teacher, partly fragments of a doctrine or attempts at systematic representations of the same. Though the dialect is different they present, in the form of the tales and in the manner of expression, a wonderful resemblance to the sacred writings of the Buddhists. [18] The Digambaras, on the other hand, have preserved nothing of the *Aṅga* but the names. They put in their place later systematic works, also in Prâkrit, and assert, in vindication of their different teaching, that the canon of their rivals is corrupted. In the further course of history, however, both branches of the Jainas have, like the Buddhists, in their continual battles with the Brâhmaṇs, found it necessary to make themselves acquainted with the ancient language of the culture of the latter. First the Digambara and later the Śvetâmbara began to use Sanskrit. They did not rest content with explaining their own teaching in Sanskrit works: they turned also to the secular sciences of the Brâhmaṇs. They have accomplished so much of importance, in grammar, in astronomy, as well as in some branches of letters, that they have won respect even from their enemies, and some of their works are still of importance to European science. In southern India, where they worked among the Draviḍian tribes, they also advanced the development of these languages. The Kanarese literary language and the Tamil and Telugu rest on the foundations laid by the Jaina monks. This activity led them, indeed, far from their proper goal, but it created for them an important position in the history of literature and culture.

The resemblance between the Jainas and the Buddhists, which I have had so often cause to bring forward, suggests the question, whether they are to be regarded as a branch of the latter, or whether they resemble the Buddhists merely because, as their tradition asserts, [19] they sprang from the same period and the same religious movement in opposition to Brâhmanism. This question, was formerly, and is still sometimes, answered in agreement with the first theory, pointing out the undoubted defects in it, to justify the rejection of the Jaina tradition, and even declaring it to be a late and intentional fabrication. In spite of this the second explanation is the right one, because the Buddhists themselves confirm the statements of the Jainas about their prophet. Old historical traditions and inscriptions prove the independent existence of the sect of the Jainas even during the first five centuries after Buddha's death, and among the inscriptions are some which clear the Jaina tradition not only from the suspicion of fraud but bear powerful witness to its honesty. [20]

The oldest canonical books of the Jaina, apart from some mythological additions and evident exaggerations, contain the following important notes on the life of their last prophet. [21] Vardhamâna was the younger son of Siddhârtha a nobleman who belonged to the Kshatriya race, called in Sanskrit Jñâti or Jñâta, in Prakrit Nâya, and, according to the old custom of the Indian warrior caste, bore the name of a Brâhmanic family the Kâśyapa. His mother, who was called Triśalâ, belonged to the family of the governors of Videha. Siddhârtha's residence was Kuṇḍapura, the Basukund of to-day, a suburb of the wealthy town of Vaiśâlî, the modern Besarh, in Videha or Tirhut. [22] Siddhârtha was son-in-law to the king of Vaiśâlî. Thirty years, it seems, Vardhamâna led a worldly life in his parents' house. He married, and his wife Yaśodâ bore him a daughter Anojjâ, who was married to a noble of the name of Jamâli, and in her turn had a daughter. In his thirty-first year his parents died. As they were followers of Pârśva the twenty-third Jina, they chose, according to the custom of the Jainas, the death of the wise by starvation. Immediately after this Vardhamâna determined to renounce the world. He got permission to take this step from his elder brother Nandivardhana, and the ruler of his land divided his possessions and became a homeless ascetic. He wandered more than twelve years, only resting during the rainy season, in the lands of the Lâḍha, in Vajjabhûmi and Subbhabhûmi, the Rârh of to-day in Bengal, and learned to bear with equanimity great hardships and cruel ill treatment at the hands of the inhabitants of those districts. Besides these he imposed upon himself the severest mortifications; after the first year he discarded clothes and devoted himself to the deepest meditation. In the thirteenth year of this wandering life he believed he had attained to the highest knowledge and to the dignity of a holy one. He then appeared as a prophet, taught the Nirgrantha doctrine, a modification of the religion of Pârśva, and organised the order of the Nirgrantha ascetics. From that time he bore the name of the venerable ascetic Mahâvîra. His career as a teacher lasted not quite thirty years, during which he travelled about, as formerly, all over the country, except during the rainy seasons. He won for himself numerous followers, both of the clergy and the lay class, among whom, however, in the fourteenth year of his period of teaching, a split arose--caused by his son-in-law Jamâli.

The extent of his sphere of influence almost corresponds with that of the kingdoms of Srâvastî or Kosala, Vidcha, Magadha, and Aṅga,--the modern Oudh, and the provinces of Tirhut and Bihâr in Western Bengal. Very frequently he spent the rainy season in his native place Vaiśâlî and in Râjagṛiha. Among his contemporaries were, a rival teacher Gosâla the son of Maṁkhali--whom he defeated in a dispute, the King of Videha--Bhambhasâra or Bibbhisâra called Sreṇika, and his sons Abhayakumâra and the parricide Ajátaśatru or Kûṇika, who protected him or accepted his doctrine, and also the nobles of the Lichchhavi and Mallaki races. The town of Pâpâ or Pâvâ, the modern Padraona [23] is given as the place of his death, where he dwelt during the rainy season of the last year of his life, in the house of the scribe of king Hastipâla. Immediately after his death, a second split took place in his community. [24]

On consideration of this information, it immediately strikes one, that the scene of Vardhamâna's activity is laid in the same part of India as Buddha laboured in, and that several of the personalities which play a part in the history of Buddha also appear in the Jaina legend. It is through the kingdoms of Kosala, Videha and Magadha, that Buddha is said to have wandered preaching, and their capitals Śrâvastî and Râjagṛiha are just the places named, where he founded the largest communities. It is also told of the inhabitants of Vaiśâlî that many turned to his doctrine. Many legends are told of his intercourse and friendship with Bimbisâra or Śreṇika, king of Videha, also of the murder of the latter by his son Ajâtaśatru, who, tortured with remorse, afterwards approached Buddha; mention is also made of his brother Abhayakumâra, likewise Makkhali Gosâla is mentioned among Buddha's opponents and rivals. It is thus clear that the oldest Jaina legend makes Vardhamâna a fellow countryman and contemporary of Buddha, and search might be suggested in the writings of the Buddhists for confirmation of these assumptions. Such indeed are to be found in no small number.

Even the oldest works of the Singalese Canon,--which date apparently from the beginning of the second century after Buddha's death, or the fourth century B.C., and which at any rate had their final edition in the third,--frequently mention an opposing sect of ascetics, the Nigaṇṭha, which the northern texts, written in

Sanskrit, recognise among the opponents of Buddha, under the name Nirgrantha, whom an old *Sûtra* [25] describes as "heads of companies of disciples and students, teachers of students, well known, renowned, founders of schools of doctrine, esteemed as good men by the multitude". Their leader is also named; he is called in Pâli Nâtaputta, in Sanskrit Jñâtiputra, that is the son of Jñâti or Nâta. The similarity between these words and the names of the family Jñâti, Jñâta or Naya, to which Vardhamâna belonged is apparent. Now since in older Buddhist literature, the title 'the son of the man of the family N. N.' is very often used instead of the individual's name, as for example, 'the son of the Sâkiya' is put for Buddha-Sâkiyaputta, so that it is difficult not to suppose that Nâtaputta or Jñâtiputra, the leader of the Nigaṇṭha or Nirgrantha sect, is the same person as Vardhamâna, the descendant of the Jñâti family and founder of the Nirgrantha or Jaina sect. If we follow up this idea, and gather together the different remarks of the Buddhists about the opponents of Buddha, then it is apparent that his identity with Vardhamâna is certain. A number of rules of doctrine are ascribed to him, which are also found among the Jainas, and some events in his life, which we have already found in the accounts of the life of Vardhamâna, are related.

In one place in the oldest part of the Singalese canon, the assertion is put into the mouth of Nigaṇṭha Nâtaputta, that the *Kiriyâvâda*--the doctrine of activity, separates his system from Buddha's teaching. We shall certainly recognise in this doctrine, the rule of the *Kiriyâ*, the activity of souls, upon which Jainism places so great importance. [26] Two other rules from the doctrine of souls are quoted in a later work, not canonical: there it is stated, in a collection of false doctrines which Buddha's rivals taught, that Nigaṇṭha asserts that cold water was living. Little drops of water contained small souls, large drops, large souls. Therefore he forbade his followers, the use of cold water. It is not difficult, in these curious rules to recognise the Jaina dogma, which asserts the existence of souls, even in the mass of lifeless elements of earth, water, fire, and wind. This also proves, that the Nigaṇṭha admitted the classification of souls, so often ridiculed by the Brâhmaṇs, which distinguishes between great and small. This work, like others, ascribes to Nigaṇṭha the assertion, that the so-called three *daṇḍa*--the three instruments by which man can cause injury to creatures--thought, word, and body, are separate active causes of sin. The Jaina doctrine agrees also in this case, which always specially represents the three and prescribes for each a special control. [27]

Besides these rules, which perfectly agree with one another, there are still two doctrines of the Nigaṇṭha to be referred to which seem to, or really do, contradict the Jainas; namely, it is stated that Nâtaputta demanded from his disciples the taking of four, not as in Vardhamâna's case, of five great vows. Although this difficulty may seem very important at first glance, it is, however, set aside by an oft repeated assertion in the Jaina works. They repeatedly say that Pàrśva, the twenty-third Jina only recognised four vows, and Vardhamâna added the fifth. The Buddhists have therefore handed down a dogma which Jainism recognises. The question is merely whether they or the Jainas are the more to be trusted. If the latter, and it is accepted that Vardhamâna was merely the reformer of an old religion, then the Buddhists must be taxed with an easily possible confusion between the earlier and later teachers. If, on the other hand, the Jaina accounts of their twenty-third prophet are regarded as mythical, and Vardhamâna is looked upon as the true founder of the sect,--then the doctrine of the four vows must be ascribed to the latter, and we must accept as a fact that he had changed his views on this point. In any case, however, the Buddhist statement speaks for, rather than against, the identity of Nigaṇṭha with Jina. [28]

Vardhamâna's system, on the other hand, is quite irreconcilable with Nâtaputta's assertion that virtue as well as sin, happiness as well as unhappiness is unalterably fixed for men by fate, and nothing in their destiny can be altered by the carrying out of the holy law. It is, however, just as irreconcilable with the other Buddhist accounts of the teaching of their opponent; because it is absolutely unimaginable, that the same man, who lays vows upon his followers, the object of which is to avoid sin, could nevertheless make virtue and sin purely dependent upon the disposition of fate, and preach the uselessness of carrying out the law. The accusation that Nâtaputta embraced fatalism must therefore be regarded as an invention and an outcome of sect hatred as well as of the wish to throw discredit on their opponents. [29]

The Buddhist remarks on the personality and life of Nâtaputta are still more remarkable. They say repeatedly that he laid claim to the dignity of an Arhat and to omniscience which the Jainas also claim for their prophet, whom they prefer simply to call 'the Arhat' and who possesses the universe-embracing '*Kevala*' knowledge. [30] A history of conversions, tells us further that Nâtaputta and his disciples disdained to cover their bodies; we are told just the same of Vardhamâna. [31] A story in the oldest part of the Singalese canon gives an interesting and important instance of his activity in teaching. Buddha, so the legend runs, once came to the town Vaiśâlî, the seat of the Kshatriya of the Lichchhavi race. His name, his law, his community were highly praised by the nobles of the Lichchhavi in the senate-house. Sîha, their general, who was a follower of the Nigaṇṭha, became anxious to know the great teacher. He went to his master Nâtaputta, who happened to be staying in Vaiśâlî just then, and asked permission to pay the visit. Twice Nâtaputta refused him. Then Sîha determined to disobey him. He sought Buddha out, heard his teaching and was converted by him. In order to show his attachment to his new teacher he invited Buddha and his disciples to eat with him. On the acceptance of the invitation, Sîha commanded his servants to provide flesh in honour of the occasion. This fact came to the ears of the followers of the Nigaṇṭha. Glad to have found an occasion to damage Buddha, they hurried in great numbers through the town, crying out, that Sîha had caused a great ox to be killed for Buddha's entertainment; that Buddha had eaten of the flesh of the animal although he knew it had been killed on his account, and was, therefore guilty of the death of the animal. The accusation was brought to Siha's notice and was declared by him to be a calumny. Buddha, however preached a sermon after the meal, in which he forbade his disciples to partake of the flesh of such animals as had been killed on their account. The legend also corroborates the account in the Jaina works, according to which Vardhamâna often resided in Vaiśâlî and had a strong following in that town. It is probably related to show that his sect was stricter, as regards the eating of flesh, than the Buddhists, a point, which again agrees with the statutes of the Jainas. [32]

The account of Nâtaputta's death is still more important. "Thus I heard it", says an old book of the Singalese canon, the *Sâmagâma Sutta*, "once the Venerable one lived in Sâmagâma in the land of the Sâkya. At that time, however, certainly the Nigaṇṭha Nâtaputta had died in Pâvâ. After his death the Nigaṇṭha wandered about disunited, separate, quarrelling, fighting, wounding each other with words." [33] Here we have complete confirmation of the statement of the Jaina canon as to the place where Vardhamâna entered *Nirvâṇa*, as well as of the statement that a schism occurred immediately after his death.

The harmony between the Buddhist and Jaina tradition, as to the person of the head of the Nirgrantha is meanwhile imperfect. It is disturbed by the description of Nâtaputta as a member of the Brâhmanic sect of the Âgniveśyâyana, whilst Vardhamâna belonged to the Kâśyapa. The point is however so insignificant, that an error on the part of the Buddhists is easily possible. [34] It is quite to be understood that perfect exactness is not to be expected among the Buddhists or any other sect in describing the person of a hated enemy. Enmity and scorn, always present, forbid that. The most that one can expect is that the majority and most important of the facts given may agree.

This condition is undoubtedly fulfilled in the case on hand. It cannot, therefore be denied, that, in spite of this difference, in spite also of the absurdity of one article of the creed ascribed to him, Vardhamâna Jñâtiputra, the founder of the Nirgrantha--or Jaina community is none other than Buddha's rival. From Buddhist accounts in their canonical works as well as in other books, it may be seen that this rival was a dangerous and influential one, and that even in Buddha's time his teaching had spread considerably. Their legends about conversions from other sects very often make mention of Nirgrantha sectarians, whom Buddha's teaching or that of his disciples had alienated from their faith. Also they say in their descriptions of other rivals of Buddha, that these, in order to gain esteem, copied the Nirgrantha and went unclothed, or that they were looked upon by the people as Nirgrantha holy ones, because they happened to have lost their clothes. Such expressions would be inexplicable if Vardhamâna's community had not become of great importance. [35]

This agrees with several remarks in the Buddhist chronicles, which assert the existence of the Jainas in different districts of India during the first century after Buddha's death. In the memoirs of the Chinese Buddhist and pilgrim Hiuen Tsiang, who visited India in the beginning of the seventh century of our era, is to be found an extract from the ancient annals of Magadha, which proves the existence of the Nirgrantha or Jainas in their original home from a very early time. [36] This extract relates to the building of the great monastry at Nâlandâ, the high school of Buddhism in eastern India, which was founded shortly after Buddha's *Nirvâṇa*, and mentions incidentally that a Nirgrantha who was a great astrologer and prophet had prophesied the future success of the new building. At almost as early a period the *Mahâvan[g]sa*, composed in the fifth century A.D., fixes the appearance of the Nirgrantha in the island of Ceylon. It is said that the king Paṇḍukâbhaya, who ruled in the beginning of the second century after Buddha, from 367-307 B.C. built a temple and a monastery for two Nirgranthas. The monastery is again mentioned in the same work in the account of the reign of a later king Vaṭṭâgâmini, cir. 38-10 B.C. It is related that Vaṭṭâgâmini being offended by the inhabitants, caused it to be destroyed after it had existed during the reigns of twenty one kings, and erected a Buddhist Saṅghârâma in its place. The latter piece of information is found also in the *Dîpavan[g]sa* of more than a century earlier. [37]

None of these works can indeed be looked upon as a truly historical source. There are, even in those paragraphs which treat of the oldest history after Buddha's death, proofs enough that they simply hand down a faulty historical tradition. In spite of this, their statements on the Nirgrantha, cannot be denied a certain weight, because they are closely connected on the one side with the Buddhist canon, and on the other they agree with the indisputable sources of history, which relate to a slightly later period.

The first authentic information on Vardhamâna's sect is given by our oldest inscriptions, the religious edicts of the Maurya king Aśoka, who, according to tradition was anointed in the year 219 after Buddha's death, and--as the reference to his Grecian contemporaries, Antiochos, Magas, Alexander, Ptolemaeus and Antigonas confirms,--ruled, during the second half of the third century B.C. over the whole of India with the exception of the Dekhan. This prince interested himself not only in Buddhism, which he professed in his later years, but he took care, in a fatherly way, as he repeatedly relates, of all other religious sects in his vast kingdom. In the fourteenth year of his reign, he appointed officials, called law-superintendents, whose duty it was to watch over the life of the different communities, to settle their quarrels, to control the distribution of their legacies and pious gifts. He says of them in the second part of the seventh 'pillar' edict, which he issued in the twenty-ninth year of his reign, "My superintendents are occupied with various charitable matters, they are also engaged with all sects of ascetics and householders; I have so arranged that they will also be occupied with the affairs of the *Saṁgha*; likewise I have arranged that they will be occupied with the Âjîvika Brâhmaṇs; I have arranged it that they will also be occupied with the Nigaṇṭha". [38] The word *Saṁgha* serves here as usual for the Buddhist monks. The Âjívikas, whose name completely disappears later, are often named in the sacred writings of the Buddhists and the Jainas as an influential sect. They enjoyed the special favour of Aśoka, who, as other inscriptions testify, caused several caves at Baràbar to be made into dwellings for their ascetics. [39] As in the still older writings of the Buddhist canon, the name Nigaṇṭha here can refer only to the followers of Vardhamâna. As they are here, along with the other two favourites, counted worthy of special mention, we may certainly conclude that they were of no small importance at the time. Had they been without influence and of small numbers Aśoka would hardly have known of them, or at least would not have singled them out from the other numerous nameless sects of which he often speaks. It may also be supposed that they were specially numerous in their old home, as Aśoka's capital Pâṭaliputra lay in this land. Whether they spread far over these boundaries, cannot be ascertained.

On the other hand we possess two documents from the middle of the next century which prove that they advanced into south-eastern India as far as Kaliṅga. These are the inscriptions at Khaṇḍagiri in Orissa, of the great King Khâravela and his first wife, who governed the east coast of India from the year 152 to 165 of the Maurya era that is, in the first half of second century B.C.

The larger inscription, unfortunately very much disfigured, contains an account of the life of Khâravela from his childhood till the thirteenth year of his reign. It begins with an appeal to the Arhat and Siddha, which corresponds to the beginning of the five-fold form of homage still used among the Jainas, and mentions the building of temples in honour of the Arhat as well as an image of the first Jina, which was taken away by a hostile king. The second and smaller inscription asserts that Khâravela's wife caused a cave to be prepared for the ascetics of Kalinga, "who believed on the Arhat." [40]

From a somewhat later period, as the characters show, from the first century B.C. comes a dedicatory inscription which has been found far to the west of the original home of the Jainas, in Mathurà on the Jamnâ. It tells of the erection of a small temple in honour of the Arhat Vardhamâna, also of the dedication of seats for the teachers, a cistern, and a stone table. The little temple, it says, stood beside the temple of the guild of tradesmen, and this remark proves, that Mathurâ, which, according to the tradition of the Jainas, was one of the chief scats of their religion, possessed a community of Jainas even before the time of this inscription. [41]

A large member of dedicatory inscriptions have come to light, which are dated from the year 5 to 98 of the era of the Indo-Skythian kings, Kanishka, Huvishka, and Vâsudeva (Bazodeo) and therefore belong at latest to the end of the first and to the second century A.D. They are all on the pedestals of statues, which are recognisable partly by the special mention of the names of Vardhamâna and the Arhat Mahâvíra, partly by absolute nudity and other marks. They show, that the Jaina community continued to flourish in Mathurâ and give besides extraordinarily important information, as I found in a renewed research into the ancient history of the sect. In a number of them, the dedicators of the statues give not only their own names, but also those of the religious teachers to whose communities they belonged. Further, they give these teachers their official titles, still used among the Jainas: *vâchaka*, 'teacher', and *gaṇin*, 'head of a school'. Lastly they specify the names of the schools to which the teachers belonged, and those of their subdivisions. The schools are called, *gaṇa*, 'companies'; the subdivisions, *kula*, 'families' and *śâkhà*, 'branches'. Exactly the same division into *gaṇa, śâkhà*, and *kula* is found in a list in one of the canonical works, of the Śvetâmbaras, the *Kalpasûtra*, which gives the number of the patriarchs and of the schools founded by them, and it is of the highest importance, that, in spite of mutilation and faulty reproduction of the inscriptions, nine of the names, which appear in the *Kalpasûtra* are recognisable in them, of which part agree exactly, part, through the fault of the stone-mason or wrong reading by the copyist, are somewhat defaced. According to the *Kalpasûtra*, Sushita, the ninth successor to Vardhamâna In the position of patriarch, together with his companion Supratibuddha, founded the 'Koḍiya' or 'Kautika *gaṇa*, which split up into four '*sâkhà*, and four '*kula*'. Inscription No. 4. which is dated in the year 9 of the king Kanishka or 87. A.D. (?) gives us a somewhat ancient form of the name of the *gaṇa Koṭiya* and that of one of its branches exactly corresponding to the *Vairi śàkhâ*. Mutilated or wrongly written, the first word occurs also in inscriptions Nos. 2, 6 and 9 as *koto-, keṭṭiya*, and *ka* ..., the second in No. 6 as *Vorâ*. One of the families of this *gaṇa*, the *Vâṇiya kula* is mentioned in No. 6, and perhaps in No. 4. The name of a second, the *Praśnavàhaṇaka*, seems to have appeared in No. 19. The last inscription mentions also another branch of the Koṭiya gaṇa, the *Majhimâ sâkhâ*, which, according to the *Kalpasûtra,* was founded by Priyagantha the second disciple of Susthita. Two still older schools which, according to tradition, sprang from the fourth disciple of the eighth patriarch, along with some of their divisions appear in inscriptions Nos. 20 and 10. These are the *Aryya-Udehikîya gaṇa*, called the school of the Ârya-Rohaṇa in the *Kalpasûtra*, to which belonged the *Parihâsaka kula* and the *Pûrnapâtrikâ śâkhâ,* as also the *Charâṇa gaṇa* with the *Prîtidharmika kula.* Each of these names is, however, somewhat mutilated by one or more errata in writing. [42] The statements in the inscriptions about the teachers and their schools are of no small importance in themselves for the history of the Jainas. If, at the end of the first century A.D.(?) many separate schools of Jaina ascetics existed, a great age and lively activity, as well as great care as regards the traditions of the sect, may be inferred. The agreement of the inscriptions with the *Kalpasûtra* leads still further however: it proves on the one side that the Jainas of Mathurâ were Śvetâmbara, and that the schism, which split the sect into two rival branches occurred long before the beginning of our era. On the other hand it proves that the tradition of the Svetâmbara really contains ancient historic elements, and by no means deserves to be looked upon with distrust. It is quite probable that, like all traditions, it is not altogether free from error. But it can no longer be declared to be the result of a later intentional misrepresentation, made in order to conceal the dependence of Jainism on Buddhism. It is no longer possible to dispute its authenticity with regard to those points which are confirmed by independent statements of other sects, and to assert, for example, that the Jaina account of the life of Vardhamâna, which agrees with the statements of the Buddists, proves nothing as regards the age of Jainism because in the late fixing of the canon of the Śvetâmbaras in the sixth century after Christ it may have been drawn from Buddhist works. Such an assertion which, under all circumstances, is a bold one, becomes entirely untenable when it is found that the tradition in question states correctly facts which lie not quite three centuries distant from Vardhamâna's time, and that the sect, long before the first century of our era kept strict account of their internal affairs. [43]

Unfortunately the testimony to the ancient history of the Jainas, so far as made known by means of inscriptions, terminates here. Interesting as it would be to follow the traces of their communities in the later inscriptions, which become so numerous from the fifth century A.D. onwards and in the description of his travels by Hiuen Tsiang, who found them spread through the whole of India and even beyond its boundaries, it would be apart from our purpose. The documents quoted suffice, however, to confirm the assertion that during the first five centuries after Buddha's death both the statements of Buddhist tradition and real historical sources give evidence to the existence of the Jainas as an important religious community independent of Buddhism, and that there are among the historical sources some which entirely clear away the suspicion that the tradition of the Jainas themselves is intentionally falsified.

The advantage gained for Indian history from the conclusion that

Jainism and Buddhism are two contemporary sects--having arisen in the same district,--is no small one. First, this conclusion shows that the religious movement of the sixth and fifth centuries B.C. in eastern India must have been a profound one. If not only one, but certainly two, and perhaps more reformers, appeared at the same time, preaching teachers, who opposed the existing circumstances in the same manner, and each of whom gained no small number of followers for their doctrines, the desire to overthrow the Brahmanical order of things must have been generally and deeply felt. This conclusion shows then that the transformation of the religious life in India was not merely the work of a religious community. Many strove to attain this object although separated from one another. It is now recognisable, though preliminarily, in one point only, that the religious history of India from the fifth century B.C. to the eighth or ninth A.D. was not made up of the fight between Brahmanism and Buddhism alone. This conclusion allows us, lastly, to hope that the thorough investigation of the oldest writings of the Jainas and their relations with Buddhism on the one hand and with Brahmanism on the other will afford many important ways of access to a more exact knowledge concerning the religious ideas which prevailed in the sixth and fifth centuries B.C., and to the establishment of the boundaries of originality between the different systems.

APPENDIX A.

Copies of the mutilated inscriptions referred to, were published by General Sir A. Cunningham in his *Archaeological Survey Reports*, vol. III, plates xiii-xv. Unfortunately they have been presented from 'copies' and are therefore full of errors, which are due for the most part, doubtless, to the copyist and not to the sculptor. It is not difficult, however, in most cases under consideration here, to restore the correct reading. Usually only vowel signs are omitted or misread and, here, and there, consonants closely resembling one another as *va* and *cha, va*, and *dha, ga* and *śa, la* and *na* are interchanged.

The formulae of the inscriptions are almost universally the same. First comes the date, then follows the name of a reverend teacher, next, the mention of the school and the subdivision of it to which he belonged. Then the persons, who dedicated the statues are named (mostly women), and who belonged to the community of the said teacher. The description of the gift forms the conclusion. The dialect of the inscriptions shows that curious mixture of Sanskṛĭt and Prâkṛĭt which is found in almost all documents of the Indo-Skythian kings, and whichas Dr. Hoernle was the first to recognise--was one of the literary languages of northern and northwestern India during the first centuries before and after the commencement of our era.

In the calculation of dates, I use the favourite starting point for the era of the Indo-Skythian kings, which unfortunately, is not certainly determined, and assume that it is identical with the *Saka* era of 78-¼ A.D. The rule of these princes could not have fallen later: in my opinion it was somewhat earlier [44] I give here transcripts and restorations of such inscriptions as mention Jaina schools or titles.

1. The inscription which is the most important for my purpose and at the same time one of the best preserved, is Sir A. Cunningham's No. 6, plate xiii, which was found on the base of a Jaina image (*Arch. Sur. Rep.* vol. III, p. 31). The copy compared with a rubbing gives the following reading, (the letters within parentheses are damaged):

L. 1. *Siddhaṁ saṁ 20 gramâ 1 di 10 + 5 ko(ṭi)yato gaṇato (Vâ)ṇiyato kulato V(ai)r(i)to śâkâto Śirikâto*

2. *(bha)ttito vâchakasya Aryya-Saṅghasihasya nir(v)varttanaṁ Dattilasya.... Vi.-*

3. *lasya ko(ṭhu)bi(ki)ya Jayavâlasya Devadâsasya Nâgadinasya cha Nâgadinâye cha (mâ)tu.*

4. *śrâ(vi)kâye (D)i-*

5. *(nâ)ye dânaṁ. i*

6. *Varddhamâna pra-*

7. *timâ|*

The lacuna in line 2, after *Dattilasya*, probably contained the word *duhituye* or *dhûtuye* and part of a male name of which only the letter *vi* is visible. In l. 3, possibly *koṭhabiniye* is to be read instead of *koṭhubikiye*. As there is room for one more letter at the end of the line, I propose to read *mâtuye*. In l. 5, *Dinâye* would stand for *Dattâyâh[postvocalic]* and be the genitive of a female name *Dinnâ* or *Dattâ*, which has been shortened *bhâmâvat*. There can be no doubt that the word *śrî*, or *śiri*, which is required, has stood before *Vardhamâna*. With these restorations the translation is as follows:

> "Success! The year 20, summer (*month*) I, day 15. An image of glorious Vardhamâna, the gift of the female lay-disciple Dinâ [*i.e.* Dinnâ or Dattâ] , the [*daughter*] of Attila, the wife of Vi..la, the mother of Jayavâla [Jayapâla] , of Devadâsa and Nâgadina [*i. e.* Nâgadinna or Nâgadatta] and of Nâgadina [*i.e.* of Nâgadinnâ or Nâgadattâ] --(*this statue being*) the *nirvartana* [45] of the preacher Aryya-Saṅghasiha [*i.e.* Ârya-Saṅghasiṁha] , out of the Koṭiya school, the Vâniya race, the Vairi branch, the Śirikâ division".

The inscription given *Arch. Sur. Rep*. vol. XX, plate v, No. 6 reads, according to an excellent rubbing:

L. 1. *Namo Arahaṁtânain namo Siddhâna saṁ* 60 [46] + 2

2. *gra 3 di 5 etâye purvâye Rârakasya Aryakakasaghastasya*

3. *śishyâ Âtapikogahabaryasya nirvartana chatnuvarnasya saṁghasya*

4. *yâ dinnâ paṭibhâ[bho?] ga* 1 (?) | (?) *Vaihikâya datti*|

"Adoration to the Arhats, adoration to the Siddhas! The year 62, the summer (*month*) 3, the day 5; on the above date a *yâ.* was given to the community, which includes four classes, as an enjoyment (*or* one share for each) (*this being*) the *nirvartana* of Atapikogahabarya, the pupil of Arya-Kakasaghasta (Ârya-Karkaśagharshita), a native of Rârâ (Râḍhâ). The gift of Vaihikâ (*or*, Vaihitâ)."

2. With the inscription No. 6 of the year 20, No. 4 (plate xiii) agrees; it was also found on a Jaina pedestal. With better readings from a rubbing of the first side only, I propose for the other portions, of which I have no rubbings, the following emendations,--l. 1, *Vâniyato kulato, sâkhâto*; l. 2, *kuṭumbimye;* I also note that the lacuna in line 2, 3th and 4th sides, would be filled exactly by *ye śrî-Vardhamânasya pratimâ kâritâ sarvasattvâ.* The former existence of the first and last seven letters may be considered certain. My restoration of the whole is,--

L. 1 (1st side) *Siddhaṁ mahârâjasya Kanishkasya râjye saṁvatsare navame* [47] (2nd side).. *mâsc pratha* 1 *divase* 5 *a-(3rd)[syâṁ] purvv[â]ye Koṭiyato gaṇato Vâniya[to]* (4th) *[ku] lato Vairito śâkâto vâchaka-*

2. (1st side) *[sya] [N]âganaṃdisa ni[rva]r[ta]naṁ Brah[ma] ... [dhû-(2nd)tuye] Bhaṭṭumitasa kuṭu[ṁ]bi[n]i[ye] Vikaṭâ-(3rd)[ye śrî Vardhamânasya pratimâ kâritâ sarva-*(4th) *satvâ] naṁ hita-*

3. *[sukhâye]* ;

and the translation:--

"Success! During the reign of the great king Kanishka, in the ninth year, 9, in the first month, 1, of ..., on the day 5,--on

> the above date [an image of glorious Vardhamâna has been caused to be made] for the welfare [and happiness] of [all created beings] by Vikatâ, the house-wife of Bhaṭṭimita (Bhattṭimitra) and [daughter of] Brâhma ...--(this statue being) the *nirvartana* of the preacher Nâganaṁidi, out of the Koṭiya school (*gaṇa*), the Vâṇiya line (*kula*), (and) the Vairi branch (*śâkhâ*)."

If we now turn to the *Kalpasûtra*, we find that Suṭṭhiya or Susthita, the eighth successor of Vardhamâna, founded the Kauṭika or Koḍiya gaṇa, which split up into four śâkhâs and four kulas. The third of the former was the Vajrî or Vairî, and the third of the latter was the Vâṇîya or Vâṇijja. It is evident that the names of the *gaṇa, kula*, and *śâkhâ* agree with those mentioned in the two inscriptions, Koṭiya being a somewhat older form of Koḍiya. But it is interesting to note that the further subdivision of the Vairî śâkhâ--the Śirikâ bhatti (Srikâ bhakti) which inscription No. 6 mentions, is not known to the *Kalpasûtra*. This is a gap such as may by be expected to occur in a list handed down by oral tradition.

3. The Koṭika gaṇa is again mentioned in the badly mutilated inscription No. 19, plate xv. A complete restoration is impossible.

> L. 1. *Saṁvalsare 90 va...sya kuṭubani. vadânasya vodhuya...*
>
> 2. *K|oṭiyato| gaṇato |Praśna|vâha|na|kato kulato Majhamâto śâkhâto...sa nikâye bhati gâlâe thabâni...*

It may, however, be inferred from the fragments of the first line that the dedication was made by a woman who was described as the wife (*kuṭumbinî*) of one person and as the daughter-in-law (*vadhu*) of another. The first part of line 2, restored as above gives--"in the congregation of ... out of the Koṭiya school, the Praśnavâhanaka line and the Majhamâ branch...." The restoration of the two names Koṭiya and Praśnavâhanaka seems to me absolutely certain, because they exactly fill the blanks in the inscription, and because the information in the *Kalpasûtra* (S. B. E. vol. XXII, p. 293) regarding the Madhyamâśâkhâ points in that direction. The latter work tells us that Priyagantha, the second pupil of Susthita and Supratibuddha, founded a śâkhâ, called Madhyamâ or Majhimâ.

As our inscriptions show that Professor Jacobi's explanation of the terms *gaṇa, kula* and *śâkhâ* [48] is correct and that the first denotes the school, the second the line of teachers, and the third a branch which separated from such a line, it follows that the śâkhâs named in the *Kalpasûtra* without the mention of a *gaṇa* and *kula*, must belong to the last preceding *gaṇa* and derive their origin from one of its *kulas*. Hence the Madhyamâ śâkhâ doubtless was included in the Kauṭika gaṇa, and an offshoot of one of its *kulas*, the fourth of which is called Praśnavâhanaka or Paṇhavâhaṇaya. The correctness of these inferences is proved by Râjaśckhara's statement regarding his spiritual descent at the end of the *Prabandha kosha*, which he composed in Vik. saṁ 1405. He informs us that he belonged to the Koṭika gaṇa, the Praśnavâhana kula, the Madhyamâ śâkhâ, the Harshapurîya gachha and the Maladhâri samtâna, founded by the illustrious Abhayasûri.

For the last words of l. 2 I do not dare to propose an emendation; I merely note that the gift seems to have consisted of pillars, *thabâni*, i. e. *stambhâh[postvocalic]*.

4. The Koṭiya gaṇa seems finally to be mentioned in pl. xiii, No. 2, where the copy of line 1, 2nd side may be corrected as,--

> *Siddha--sa 5 he 1 di 10 + 2 asyâ purvvâye Koṭ(iya).*

5. Names of an older *gaṇa* and of one of its *kulas* occur in No. 10 plate xiv, where the copy, which is faulty, may allow the following partial restoration,---

> L. 1. *Sa 40 + 7 gra 2 di 20 etasyâ purvvâye Vâraṇe gaṇe Petidhamikakulavâchakasya Rohanadisya sîsasya Senasya nivatanam sâvaka-Da*
>
> 2. *...pashâṇavadhaya Giha..ka.bha.. prapâ [di] nâ..mâ ta...*

which I translate--

> "The year 47, the summer (month) 2, the day 20,--on the above date a drinking fountain was given by ..., the ... of the

lay-disciple Da ... (this being) the *nivatana* of Sena the pupil of Rohanadi (Rohanandi) and preacher of the Petidhamika (Praitidharmika) line, in the Vâraṇa school."

Varane must be a mistake for the very similar word *Chârane*. The second *kula* of this *gaṇa* which, according to the *Kalpasûtra* (*S.B.E.* vol. XXII, p. 291) was founded by Śrîgupta, the fifth pupil of Ârya Suhastin, is the Prîtidharmika (p. 292). It is easy to see that a similar name is hidden in the compound *Petivamikakutavâchakasya* 'of the preacher of the Petivâmika line'; and an inscription excavated by Dr. Fuhrer at Mathurâ mentions the Petivâmika (*kula*) of the Vârana *gaṇa*. With the second line little can be done: if the letters *prapâ* are correct and form a word, one of the objects dedicated must have been a drinking fountain.

6. The inscription No. 20, plate xv offers likewise slightly corrupt and mutilated names of a *gaṇa*, a *kula* and a *sâkhâ*, mentioned in the *Kalpasûtra*. In the lithographed copy lines 3-7 are hopeless and there is no rubbing to help. The word *thitu* 'of a daughter' in line 6, and the following *ma.uya* which is probably a misreading of *mâtuye* 'of the mother' show that this dedication also was made by a female. The last four syllables *vato maho* are probably the remnant of another namaskâra--*namo bhagavato Mahâvîrasya.* As regards the proper names, Aryya Rehiniya is an impossible form; but on comparison with the next inscription to be mentioned, it is evident that the stone must have read *Aryvodchikiyâto* or *Aryyadehikiyâto g>ṇâ[to]* . [49] According to the *Kalpasûtra* (*S.B.E.* vol. XXII, p. 291) Ârya-Rohaṇa was the first pupil of Ârya Suhastin and founded the Uddeha gaṇa. The latter split up into four śâkhâs and into six kulas. The name of its fourth śâkhâ, Pûrṇapatrikâ, closely resembles--especially in its consonantal elements--that of the inscription, *Petaputrikâ*, and I do not hesitate in correcting the latter to *Ponapatrikâ* which would be the equivalent of Sansk. Paurṇapatrikâ. Among the six kulas is the Parihâsaka, and considering the other agreements, I believe it probable that the mutilated name read as *Puridha.ka* is a misreading of *Parihâka*, We may emend the first two times and read as follows,--

L. 1. *Siddha|m| namo arahato Mahâvir|a|sya devanâśasya | râjña Vâsudevasya saṁvatsare 90 + 8 varshamâse + divase*

10 | 1 etasyâ.

2. *purvv|â|y|e| Aryyo-D|e|h|i|kiyâto gaṇâ[|to| P|a|vi|hâsa|k|a|kula|to| P|ou|ap|a|trikât|o| śâkâto gaṇ|i|sya Aryya-Devadatta|sya| na... ...*

3. *ryya-Kshemasya*

4. *prakagiriṇe*

5. *kihadiye prajâ*

6. *tasya Pravarakasya dhitu Varaṇasya gatvakasya ma|t|uya Mitra(?)sa ...datta gâ*

7. *ye..|namo bhaga|vato mah|âvîrasya|*

and the translation (so far) will be,--

> "Success! Adoration to the Arhat Mahâvirâ, the destroyer(?) of the gods. In the year of king Vâsudeva, 98, in the month 4 of the rainy season, on the day 11--on the above date ... of the chief of the school (*gaṇin*) Aryya-Devadata (Devadatta) out of the school (*gaṇa*) of the Aryya-Udehikîya (Ârya-Uddehikiya), out of the Parihâsaka line (*kula*), out of the Ponapatrikâ (Paurṇapatrikâ) branch (*śâkhâ*)." [50]

These and many other statements in the inscriptions, about the teachers and their schools are of no small importance in themselves for the early history of the Jainas. The agreement of the above with the *Kalpasûtra* can best be shown by placing the statements in question against one another. The inscriptions prove the actual existence of twenty of the subdivisions mentioned in the Sthavirâvali of the *Kalpasûtra*. Among its eight gaṇas we can certainly trace three, possibly four--the Uddchika, Vâraṇa, Veśavâḍiya(?) and Koḍiya.

Inscriptions:

1. Koṭṭiya (Koḍiya)

Gana

Bramadâsika kula
Thâniya kula
P[aṇha] vahu[ṇaya] ku[la]
Majhamâ śâkhâ

Uchchenâgarî śâkhâ
Vairî, Vairiyâ śâkhâ

The Sthavirâvalî of the *Kalpasûtra (Sac. Bks. of the East*, vol. XXII, p. 292) states that Susṭhita and Supratibuddha founded the--

Koṭiya or
Kauṭaka
Gaṇa

kulas	**śâkhâs**
1. *Bambhalijja*	1. *Uchchanâgarî*
2. Vachchhalijja	2. *Vijjâharî*
3. *Vâṇîya* or *Vâṇîjja*	3. Vajrî
4. Panhavâhanaya	4. *Majjhimáka* or Praśnavâhanaka
	5. Majjhîma (scholar of the two teachers. founded by Priyagantha the second)

Inscriptions:

2. Vâraṇa Gaṇa

kulas
Petivamika
Âryya Hâṭikiya
Puśyamitrîya
Aryya-Cheṭiya
Kaniyasika

śâkhâs
Vâjanâgarî
Harîtamâlakaḍhî

The *Kalpasûtra* states that Śrîgupta of the Hâritagotra founded the Châraṇa gaṇa, which was divided into four *śâkhâs* and into seven *kulas*:

Châraṇa-gaṇa

.. . .

kulas

1. Vachchhalijja
2. *Pîdhammiya*
3. *Hâlijja*
4. *Pûsamittijja*
5. Mâlijja
6. *Ârya-Cheḍaya*
7. *Kaṇhasaha*

śâkhâs

Saṁ kâśikâ

Vajjanâgarî

Gavedhukâ

Hâriyamâlagârî

Inscriptions:

:

3. Aryya-Udekiya Gaṇa

.. . .

kulas

Nágabhatikiya

Puridha

Petaputrikâ śâkhâ

The *Kalpasûtra* says Ârya-Rohana of the Kâśyapa gotra founded the

Uddeha
Gana

.. . .

kulas

1. *Nâgabhûya*
2. Somabhûta

Udumbarijjiyâ

3. Ullagachchha (or Ârdrakachchha?)	Matipatrikâ *Puṇṇapattiyâ*
4. Ilatthilijja	
5. Nandijja	
6. *Parihâsaka*	

Inscriptions:

4. [Veśavâdiya Gaṇa] [51]

[Me] hika kula

The *Kalpasûtra*:--Kâmarddhi of the Kuṇḍalagotra founded the Veśavâṭika gaṇa which was divided into four śàkhâs, and into four kulas:--

Veśavâṭika Gaṇa

kulas	**śâkhâs**
Gaṇika	Śrâvastikâ
Maighika	Rajjapâliyâ
Kâmarddhika	Antarijjiyâ
Indrapuraka	Khemalijjiyâ

[52]

The resemblance of most of these names is so complete that no explanation is necessary.

The Indian Sect of the Jains

FOOTNOTES

Footnote 1: In notes on the Jainas, one often finds the view expressed, that the *Digambaras* belong only to the south, and the *Śvetâmbaras* to the north. This is by no means the case. The former in the Panjâb, in eastern Râjputâna and in the North West Provinces, are just as numerous, if not more so, than the latter, and also appear here and there in western Râjputâna and Gujarât: see *Indian Antiquary*, vol. VII, p. 28.

Footnote 2: The ascetics of lower rank, now called Paṇḍit, now-a-days wear the costume of the country. The Bhaṭṭâraka, the heads of the sect, usually wrap themselves in a large cloth (*chadr*). They lay it off during meals. A disciple then rings a bell as a sign that entrance is forbidden (*Ind. Ant.* loc. cit.). When the present custom first arose cannot be ascertained. From the description of the Chinese pilgrim Hiuen Tsiang (St. Julien, *Vie.* p. 224), who calls them Li-hi, it appears that they were still faithful to their principles in the beginning of the seventh century A.D. "The Li-hi (Nirgranthis) distinguish themselves by leaving their bodies naked and pulling out their hair. Their skin is all cracked, their feet are hard and chapped: like rotting trees that one sees near rivers."

Footnote 3: See below.

Footnote 4: In the stereotyped introductions to the sermons of Jina it is always pointed out that they are addressed to the Aryan and non-Aryan. Thus in the *Aupapâtika Sûtra* § 56. (Leumann) it runs as follows: *tesiṁ savvesiṁ âṛiyamanâriyanaṁ agilâe dhammatṁ âikkhai* "to all these, Aryans and non-Aryans, he taught the law untiringly". In accordance with this principle, conversions of people of low caste, such as gardeners, dyers, etc., are not uncommon even at the present day. Muhammadans too, regarded as Mlechcha, are still received among the Jaina communities. Some cases of the kind were communicated to me in Ah[postvocalic]madâbâd in the year 1876, as great triumphs of the Jainas. Tales of the conversion of the emperor Akbar, through the patriarch Hîravijaya (*Ind. Antiq.* Vol. XI, p. 256), and of the spread of the Digambara sect in an island Jainabhadri, in the Indian Ocean (*Ind. Ant.* Vol. VII, p. 28) and in Arabia, shew that the Jainas are familiar with the idea of the conversion of non-Indians. Hiuen Tsiang's note on the appearance of the Nirgrantha or Digambara in Kiapishi (Beal, *Si-yu-ki*, Vol. I, p. 55), points apparently to the fact that they had, in the North West at least, spread their missionary activity beyond the borders of India.

Footnote 5: Even the canonical works of the Śvetâmbara, as for example, the *Âchârâṅga (Sacred Books of the East*, Vol. XXII, p. 88-186) contain directions for nuns. It seems, however, that they have never played such an important part as in Buddhism. At the present time, the few female orders among the Śvetâmbara consist entirely of virgin widows, whose husbands have died in childhood, before the beginning of their life together. It is not necessary to look upon the admission of nuns among the Śvetâmbara as an imitation of Buddhist teaching, as women were received into some of the old Brahmanical orders; see my note to *Manu*, VIII, 363, (*Sac. Bks. of the East*, Vol. XXV, p. 317). Among the Digambaras, exclusion of women was demanded from causes not far to seek. They give as their reason for it, the doctrine that women are not capable of attaining *Nirvâṇa*; see Peterson, *Second Report*, in *Jour. Bom. Br. R. As. Soc.* Vol. XVII, p. 84.

Footnote 6: The titles Siddha, Buddha and Mukta are certainly borrowed by both sects from the terminology of the Brâhmaṇs, which they used, even in olden times, to describe those saved during their lifetimes and used in the Śaivite doctrine to describe a consecrated one who is on the way to redemption. An Arhat, among the Brâhmaṇs, is a man distinguished for his knowledge and pious life (comp. for example Âpastamba, *Dharmasûtra.* I, 13, 13; II, 10, I.) and this idea is so near that of the Buddhists and the Jainas that it may well be looked upon as the foundation of the latter. The meaning of Tîrthakara "prophet, founder of religion", is derived from the Brâhmanic use of *tîrtha* in the sense of "doctrine". Comp. also H. Jacobi's Article on the Title of Buddha and Jina, *Sac. Books of the East*. Vol. XXII, pp. xix, xx.

Footnote 7: A Sâgara or Sâgaropamâ of years is == 100,000,000,000,000 Palya or Palyopama. A Palya is a period in which a well, of one or, according to some, a hundred *yojana*, i.e. of one or a hundred geographical square miles, stuffed full of fine hairs, can be emptied, if one hair is pulled out every hundred years:

Wilson, *Select. Works*, Vol. I, p. 309; Colebrooke, *Essays*, Vol. II, p. 194. ed. Cowell.

Footnote 8: For the list of these Jinas, see below.

Footnote 9: More complete representations are to be found in Colebrooke's *Misc. Essays*. Vol. I, pp. 404, 413, with Cowell's Appendix p. 444-452; Vol. II, pp. 194, 196, 198-201; H. H. Wilson's *Select Works*, Vol. I, pp. 297-302, 305-317; J. Stevenson, *Kalpasûtra*, pp. xix-xxv; A. Barth, *Religions de l'Inde*, pp. 84-91.

Footnote 10: On the Jaina Paradise see below. Dr. Bühler seems here to have confounded the *Alôka* or Non-world, 'the space where only things without life are found', with the heaven of the Siddhas; but these are living beings who have crossed the boundary

Footnote 11: The Digambara sect, at least in southern India, do not seem to be all quite so punctiliously careful in this as the Śvetâmbara of western India.--Ed.

Footnote 12: On the five great vows see the *Âchârâṅga Sûtra*, II, 15: *S.B.E.* Vol. XXII, pp. 202-210. The Sanskrit terms of the Jains are: 1. *ahiṁsâ*, 2. *sûnrita*, 3. *asteya*, 4. *brahmâchârya*, 5. *aparigraha*; those of the Brahmanical ascetics: 1. *ahiṁsa*, 2. *satya*, 3. *asteya*, 4. *brahmâchârya*, 5. *tyâga*.

Footnote 13: With reference to asceticism, comp. Leumann, *Aupapâtika Sûtra* § 30. The death of the wise ones by starvation is described, Weber, *Bhagavatî Sûtra*, II, 266-267; Hoernle *Upâsakadaśa Sûtra,* pp. 44-62; *Âchârâṅga Sûtra*, in *S.B.E.* Vol. XXII, pp. 70-73. Among the Digambara the heads of schools still, as a rule, fall victims to this fate. Even among the Śvetâmbara, cases of this kind occur, see K. Forbes, *Râs Mâlâ*, Vol. II, pp. 331-332, or 2nd ed. pp. 610-611.

Footnote 14: An example may be found in Jacobi's careful comparison of the customs of the Brâhmanic and Jaina ascetics, in the beginning of his translation of the *Âchârâṅga Sûtra, S.B.E.*, Vol. XXII, pp. xxi--xxix. In relation to the death by starvation of

Brahmanical hermits and Sannyâsin, see Âpastamba, *Dharmasûtra*, in S.B.E. Vol. II, pp. 154, 156, where (IT, 22, 4 and II, 23, 2) it, says of the penitents who have reached the highest grade of asceticism: "Next he shall live on water (then) on air, then on ether".

Footnote 15: The *Upâsakadaśâ Sûtra* treats of the right life of the laity, Hoernle, pp. 11-37 (Bibl. Ind.), and Hemachandra, *Yogasûtra*, Prakâsa ii and iii; Windisch, *Zeitschrift der Deutsch Morg. Ges.* Bd. XXVIII, pp. 226-246. Both scholars have pointed out in the notes to their translations, the relationship between the precepts and terms, of the Jainas and Buddhists. The Jainas have borrowed a large number of rules directly from the law books of the Brâhmaṇs. The occupations forbidden to the Jaina laity are almost all those forbidden by the Brâhmanic law to the Brâhmaṇ, who in time of need lives like a Vaīśya. Hemachandra, *Yogaśâstra*, III, 98--112 and *Upâsakadaśâ Sûtra*, pp. 29-30, may be compared with Manu, X, 83-89, XI, 64 and 65, and the parallel passages quoted in the synopsis to my translation (*S.B.E.* Vol. XXV).

Footnote 16: For the Jaina ritual, see *Indian Antiquary*. Vol. XIII, pp. 191-196. The principal sacred places or Tirthas are--Sameta Śikhara in Western Bengal, where twenty of the Jinas are said to have attained Nirvâṇa; Śatruñjaya and Girnâr in Kâthiâwâḍ sacred respectively to Ṛishabhanâtha and Neminâtha; Chandrapuri where Vâsupûjya died; and Pâwâ in Bengal at which Vardhamâna died.--Ed.

Footnote 17: The latter assertion is to be found In the *Shaḍdarśanasamuchchaya* Vers. 45, 77-78. A creative activity is attributed to the Jinas even in the Kuhâon inscription which is dated 460-461 A.D. (*Ind. Antiq*. Vol. X, p. 126). There they are called *âdikartri* the 'original creators'. The cause of the development of a worship among the Jainas was first rightly recognised by Jacobi, *S.B.E.* Vol. XXII, p. xxi. The Jaina worship differs in one important point from that of the Buddhists. It recognised no worship of relics.

Footnote 18: A complete review of the *Aṅga* and the canonical works which were joined to it later, is to be found in A. Weber's fundamental treatise on the sacred writings of the Jainas in the *Indische Studien*, Bd. XVI, SS. 211-479 and Bd. XVIII, SS. 1-90. The *Âchârâṅga* and the *Kalpasûtra* are translated by H. Jacobi in the *S.B.E* Vol. XXII, and a part of the *Upâsakadasâ Sûtra* by R. Hoernle in the *Bibl. Ind.* In the estimates of the age of the *Aṅga* I follow H. Jacobi, who has throughly discussed the question *S.B.E.* Vol. XXII, pp. xxxix-xlvii.

Footnote 19: The later tradition of the Jainas gives for the death of their prophet the dates 545, 527 and 467 B.C. (see Jacobi, *Kalpasûtra* introd. pp. vii--ix and xxx). None of the sources in which these announcements appear are older than the twelfth century A.D. The latest is found in Hemachandra who died in the year 1172 A.D. The last is certainly false if the assertion, accepted by most authorities, that Buddha's death falls between the years 482 and 472 B.C. is correct. For the Buddhist tradition maintains that the last Jaina Tîrhakara died during Buddha's lifetime (see p. 34).

Footnote 20: Apart from the ill-supported supposition of Colebrooke, Stevenson and Thomas, according to which Buddha was a disloyal disciple of the founder of the Jainas, there is the view held by H. H. Wilson, A. Weber, and Lassen, and generally accepted till twenty-five years ago, that the Jainas are an old sect of the Buddhists. This was based, on the one hand, upon the resemblance of the Jaina doctrines, writings, and traditions to those of the Buddhists, on the other, on the fact that the canonical works of the Jainas show a more modern dialect than those of the Buddhists, and that authentic historical proofs of their early existence are wanting. I was myself formerly persuaded of the correctness of this view and even thought I recognised the Jainas in the Buddhist school of the Sammatîya. On a more particular examination of Jaina literature, to which I was forced on account of the collection undertaken for the English Government in the seventies, I found that the Jainas had changed their name and were always, in more ancient times, called Nirgrantha or Nigaṇṭha. The observation that the Buddhists recognise the Nigaṇṭha and relate of their head and founder, that he was a rival of Buddha's and died at Pâvâ where the last Tîrthakara is said to have attained *Nirvâṇa*, caused me to accept the view that the Jainas and the Buddhists sprang from the same religious movement. My supposition was confirmed by Jacobi, who reached the like view by another course, independently of mine (see *Zeitschrift der Deutsch Morg. Ges.* Bd. XXXV, S. 669. Note 1), pointing out that the last Tîrthakara in the Jaina canon bears the same name as among the Buddhists. Since the publication of our results in the *Ind. Ant.* Vol. VII, p. 143 and in Jacobi's introduction to his edition of the *Kalpasûtra,* which have been further verified by Jacobi with great penetration, views on this question have been divided. Oldenberg, Kern, Hoernle, and others have accepted this new view without hesitation, while A Weber (*Indische Studien* Bd. XVI, S. 240) and Barth (*Revue de l'Histoire des Religions*, tom. III, p. 90) keep to their former standpoint. The latter do not trust the Jaina tradition and believe it probable that the statements in the same are falsified. There are certainly great difficulties in the way of accepting such a position especially the improbability that the Buddhists should have forgotten the fact of the defection of their hated enemy. Meanwhile, this is not absolutely impossible as the oldest preserved Jaina canon had its first authentic edition only in the fifth or sixth century of our era, and as yet the proof is wanting that the Jainas, in ancient times, possessed a fixed tradition. The belief that I am able to insert this missing link in the chain of argument and the hope of removing the doubts of my two honoured friends has caused me to attempt a connected statement of the whole question although this necessitates the repetition of much that has already been said, and is in the first part almost entirely a recapitulation of the results of Jacobi's researches.

Footnote 21: The statement that Vardhamâna's father was a mighty king belongs to the manifest exaggerations. This assertion is refuted by other statements of the Jainas themselves. See Jacobi, *S.B.E.* Vol. XXII, pp. xi-xii.

Footnote 22: Dr. Bühler by a slip had here "Magadha oder Bihâr".--J. B.

Footnote 23: This is General Cunningham's identification and a probable one.--Ed.

Footnote 24: Notes on Mahâvîra's life are to be found especially in *Âchârâṅga Sûtra* in *S.B.E.* Vol. XXII, pp. 84-87, 189-202; *Kalpasûtra,* ibid. pp. 217-270. The above may be compared with Jacobi's representation, ibid. pp. x-xviii. where most of the identifications of the places named are given, and *Kalpasûtra* introd. p. ii. We have to thank Dr. Hoernle for the important information that Vardhamâna's birthplace Kuṇḍapura is still called Vasukund: *Upâsakadaśâ Sûtra* p. 4. Note 3. The information on the schisms of the Jainas is collected by Lemmann in the *Indische Studien*, Bd. XVII, S. 95 ff.

Footnote 25: The *Mahâparinibbâṇa Sutta*, in *S.B.E.* Vol. XI, p. 106.

Footnote 26: Jacobi, *Zeitschrift der Deutsch. Morg. Ges.* Bd. XXXIV, S. 187; *Ind. Antiq.* Vol. IX, p. 159.

Footnote 27: Jacobi, *Ind. Antiq.* Vol. IX, p. 159.

Footnote 28: Jacobi, *loc. cit.*. p. 160, and Leumann, *Actes du VIième Congrès Int. des Or.* Sect. Ary. p. 505. As the Jaina accounts of the teaching of Pârśva and the existence of communities of his disciples, sound trustworthy, we may perhaps accept, with Jacobi, that they rest on a historical foundation.

Footnote 29: Jacobi *loc. cit.*. p. 159-160.

Footnote 30: See for example the account in the *Chullavagga*, in *S.B.E.* Vol. XX. p. 78-79; *Ind. Antiq.* Vol. VIII, p. 313.

Footnote 31: Spence Hardy, *Manual of Budhism*, p. 225.

Footnote 32: *S.B.E.* Vol. XVII, pp. 108-117.

Footnote 33: The passage is given in the original by Oldenberg, *Leitsch. der D. Morg. Ges.* Bd. XXXIV, S. 749. Its significance in connection with the Jaina tradition as to their schisms has been overlooked until now. It has also been unnoticed that the assertion, that Vardhamâna died during Buddha's lifetime, proves that the latest account of this occurrence given by traditions 467 B.C. is false: Later Buddhist legends (Spence Hardy, *Manual of Budhism*, pp. 266-271) treat of Nâtaputta's death in more detail. In a lengthy account they give as the cause of the same the apostacy of one of his disciples, Upâli who was converted by Buddha. After going over to Buddhism, Upâli treated his former master with scorn, and presumed to relate a parable which should prove the foolishness of those who believed in false doctrines. Thereupon the Nigaṇṭha fell into despair. He declared his alms-vessel was broken, his existence destroyed, went to Pâva, and died there. Naturally no importance is to be given to this account and its details. They are apparently the outcome of sect-hatred.

Footnote 34: According to Jacobi's supposition, *S.B.E.* Vol. XXII, p. xvi, the error was caused, by the only disciple of Vardhamâna, who outlived his master, Sudharman being an Âgniveśyâyana.

Footnote 35: See for the history of Sîha related above, Spence Hardy, *Manual of Budhism*, pp. 226, 266, and Jacobi, *Ind. Antiq.* Vol. VIII, p. 161

Footnote 36: Beal, *Si-yu-ki*. Vol. II, p. 168.

Footnote 37: Turnour, *Mahâvaṅsa*, pp. 66-67 and p. 203, 206: *Dîpavan[g]sa* XIX 14; comp. also Kern, *Buddhismus*, Bd. I, S. 422. In the first passage in the *Mahâvaṅ sa*, three Nighaṇṭas are introduced by name, Jotiya, Giri, and Kumbhaṇḍa. The translation incorrectly makes the first a Brâhmaṇ and chief engineer.

Footnote 38: See Senart, *Inscriptions de Piyadasi*, tom. II, p. 82. Ed. VIII, l. 4. My translation differs from Senart's in some points especially in relation to the construction. Conf. *Epigraphia Indiea*, vol. II, pp. 272f.

Footnote 39: See *Ind. Antiquary*, vol. XX, pp. 361 ff.

Footnote 40: The meaning of these inscriptions, which were formerly believed to be Buddhist, was first made clear by Dr.

Bhangvânlâl's Indrâji's careful discussion in the *Actes du VIième Congrès Internat. des Orientalistes* Sect. Ary. pp. 135-159. H; first recognised the true names of the King Khâravela and his predecessors and shewed that Khâravela and his wife were patrons of the Jainas. We have to thank him for the information that the inscription contains a date in the Maurya Era. I have thoroughly discussed his excellent article in the *Oesterreichischen Monatsschrift*, Bd. X, S. 231 ff. and have there given my reasons for differing from him on an important point, namely, the date of the beginning of the Maurya Era, which, according to his view begins with the conquest of Kaliṅga by Aśoka about 255 B. C. Even yet I find it impossible to accept that the expression, "in the hundred and sixty fifth year of the era of the Maurya Kings", can mean anything else than that 164 years have passed between the thirteenth year of the rule of Khâravela and the anointing of the first Maurya King Chandrugupta. Unfortunately it is impossible to fix the year of the latter occurrence, or to say more than that it took place between the years 322 and 312 B.C. The date given in Khâravela's inscription cannot therefore be more closely fixed than that it lies between 156 and 147 B.C. I now add to my former remarks--that appeals to the Arhat and Siddha appear also in Jaina inscriptions from Mathurâ and may be taken as a certain mark of the sect. Thus it is worthy of note that even in Hiuen Tsiang's time, (Beal, *Si-yu-ki*, Vol. II, p. 205) Kalinga was one of the chief seats of the Jainas.

Footnote 41: This inscription also was first made known by Dr Bhagwanlal Indiaji, *loc. cit.* p. 143.

Footnote 42: Dr. Bühler's long note (p. 48) on these inscriptions was afterwards expanded in the *Wiener Zeitschrift fur die Kunde des Morgenlandes* Bd. I, S. 165-180; Bd. II, S. 141-146. Bd. III, S. 233-240; and Bd. IV, S. 169-173. The argument of these papers is summarised in. Appendix. A, pp. 48 ff.--Ed.

Footnote 43: See Weber's and Barth's opinions quoted above in note I, p. 23.

Footnote 44: What follows is from the author's later and fuller paper in *Wiener Zeitschrift für die Kunde des Morgenlandes*, Bd. I,

S. 170 f., but abridged.--Ed.

Footnote 45: The word *nirvartana* has the meaning of 'in obedience to the order', or 'in consequence of the request'. It occurs again in the Prakrit form *nivatanaṁ* below, in No. 10 (pl. xiv) and it has stood in No. 4, and at the end of l. 2 of No. 7, where the rubbing has *nirva*. It is also found in the next: *Arch. Sur. Rep.* vol. XX, pl. v, No. 6.

Footnote 46: In reading the first figure as 60, I follow Sir A. Cunningham. I have never seen the sign, in another inscription. The characters of the inscription are so archaic that this date may refer to an earlier epoch than the Indo-Skythian.

Footnote 47: *Sac. Bks. East*, vol. XXII p. 292.

Footnote 48: *S. B. E.* vol. XXII, p. 288, note 2.

Footnote 49: *Wiener Zeitshe. f. d. Kunde der Morgenl.*, Bd. II, S. 142 f.

Footnote 50: At a later date Dr. Bühler added other proofs from inscriptions of the authenticity of the Jaina tradition, in the *Vienna Oriental Journal*, vol. II, pp. 141-146; vol. III, pp. 233-240; vol. IV, pp. 169-173, 313-318; vol. V, pp. 175-180; and in *Epigraphia Indica*, vol. I pp. 371-397; vol. II, pp. 195-212, 311. The paragraphs given above are chiefly from his first paper in the *Vienna Oriental Journal* (vol. I, pp. 165-180), which appears to be an extended revision of the long footnote in the original paper on the Jainas, but it is here corrected in places from readings in his later papers.--J. B.

Footnote 51: *Epigraphia Indica*, vol. I, pp. 382, 388.

Footnote 52: For the above lists see *Wiener Zeitschi*. Bd. IV, S. 316 ff. and *Kalpasûtra* in *S. B. E.* vol. XXII, pp. 290 f.

JAINA MYTHOLOGY.

The mythology of the Jainas, whilst including many of the Hindu divinities, to which it accords very inferior positions, is altogether different in composition. It has all the appearance of a purely constructed system. The gods are classified and subdivided into orders, genera, and species; all are mortal, have their ages fixed, as well as their abodes, and are mostly distinguished by cognizances *chihnas* or *lâñchhaṇas*. Their Tîrthakaras, Tìrthamkaras, or perfected saints, are usually known as twenty-four belonging to the present age. But the mythology takes account also of a past and a future age or renovation of the world, and to each of these aeons are assigned twenty-four Tîrthakaras. But this is not all: in their cosmogony they lay down other continents besides Jambûdvîpa-Bharata or that which we dwell in. These are separated from Jambûdvîpa by impassable seas, but exactly like it in every respect and are called Dhâtuki-kanda and Pushkarârddha; and of each of these there are eastern, and western Bharata and Airàvata regions, whilst of Jambûdvîpa there is also a Bharata and an Airâvata region: these make the following ten regions or worlds:--

1. Jambûdvîpa-bharata-kshetra.
2. Dhâtukî-khaṇḍa pûrva-bharata.
3. Dhâtukî-khaṇḍa paśchima-bharata.
4. Pushkarârddha pûrva-bharata.
5. Pushkaravaradvîpa paśchima-bharata.
6. Jambûdvîpa airâvata-kshetra.
7. Dhâtukî-khaṇḍa pûrva-airâvata.
8. Dhâtukî-khaṇḍa paśchima-airâvata.
9. Pushkarârdhadvîpa pûrva-airâvata.
10. Puskarârddha paśchima-airâvata.

To each of these is allotted twenty four past, present and future Atîts or Jinas,--making in all 720 of this class, for which they have invented names: but they are only names. [1]

Of the Tîrthakaras of the present age or *avasarpini* in the Bharata-varsha of Jambûdvîpa, however, we are supplied with minute details:--their names, parents, stations, reputed ages, complexions, attendants, cognizances (*chihna*) or characteristics, etc. and these details are useful for the explanation of the iconography we meet with in the shrines of Jaina temples. There the images of the Tîrthakaras are placed on highly sculptured thrones and surrounded by other smaller attendant figures. In temples of the Śvetâmbara sect the images are generally of marble--white in most cases, but often black for images of the 19th, 2Oth, 22nd and 23rd Jinas. On the front of the throne or *âsana* are usually carved three small figures: at the proper right of the Jina is a male figure representing the Yaksha attendant or servant of that particular Jina; at the left end of the throne is the corresponding female--or Yakshinî, Yakshî or Śâsanadevî; whilst in a panel in the middle there is often another devî. At the base of the seat also, are placed nine very small figures representing the *navagraha* or nine planets; that is the sun, moon, five planets, and ascending and descending nodes.

In the Jaina *Purânas*, legends are given to account for the connexion of the Yakshas and Yakshîs with their respective Tîrthakaras: thus, in the case of Pârśvanâtha, we have a story of two brothers Marubhûti and Kamaṭha, who in eight successive incarnations were always enemies, and were finally born as Pârśvanâtha and Sambaradeva respectively. A Pâshaṇḍa or unbeliever, engaged in the *panchâgni* rite, when felling a tree for his fire, against the remonstrance of Pârśvanâtha, cut in pieces two snakes that were in it; the Jina, however restored them to life by means of the *pañchamantra*. They were then re-born in Pâtâla-loka as Dharaṇendra or Nâgendra-Yaksha and Padmâvatî-Yakshiṇî. When Sambaradeva or Meghakumâra afterwards attacked the Arbat with a great storm, whilst he was engaged in the *Kâyotsarga* austerity--standing immovable, exposed to the weather--much in the way that Mâra attacked Śâkya Buddha at Bodh-gayâ, Dharaṇendra's throne in Pâtâla thereupon shook, and the Nâga or Yaksha with his consort at once sped to the protection of his former benefactor. Dharaṇendra spread his many hoods over the head of the Arhata and the Yakshṅî Padmâvatî held a white umbrella (*śveta chhatri*) over him for protection. Ever after they became his constant attendants, just as Śakra was to Buddha. The legend is often represented in old-sculptures, in the cave-temples at Bâdâmi,

Elura, etc., and the figure of Pârśva is generally carved with the snake-hoods (*Śeshaphaṇi*) over him. [2]

Other legends account for the attachment of each pair of Śâsanadevatâs to their respective Jinas.

The Śvetâmbaras and Digambaras agree generally in the details respecting the different Tîrthakaras; but, from information furnished from Maisur, they seem to differ as to the names of the Yakshiṇis attached to the several Tîrthakaras, except the first and last two; they differ also in the names of several of the Jinas of the past and the future aeons. The Digambaras enlist most of the sixteen Vidyâdevis or goddesses of knowledge among the Yakshiṇîs, whilst the other sect include scarcely a third of them.

These Vidyâdevîs, as given by Hemachandra, are--(1) Rohiṇî; (2) Prajñaptî; (3) Vajrasṛiṅkhalâ; (4) Kuliśânkuścâ--probably the Ankuśa-Yakshî of the Śvetàmbâra fourteenth Jina; (5) Chakreśvarî; (6) Naradattâ or Purushadattâ; (7) Kâli or Kâlîkâ; (8) Mahákâlî; (9) Gaurî; (10) Gândhârî; (11) Sarvâstramahâjvâlâ; (12) Mânavî; (13) Vairoṭyâ; (14) Achchhuptâ; (15) Mânasî; and (16) Mahâmânasikâ.

The images of the Tîrthakaras are always represented seated with their legs crossed in front--the toes of one foot resting close upon the knee of the other; and the right hand lies over the left in the lap. All are represented exactly alike except that Pârśvanâtha, the twenty-third, has the snake-hoods over him; and, with the Digambaras, Supârśva--the seventh, has also a smaller group of snake hoods. The Digambara images are all quite nude; those of the Śvetâmbaras are represented as clothed, and they decorate them with crowns and ornaments. They are distinguished from one another by their attendant *Yakshas* and *Yakshiṇîs* as well as by their respective *chihnas* or cognizances which are carved on the cushion of the throne.

All the Jinas are ascribed to the Ikshvâku family (*kula*)except the twentieth Munisuvrata and twenty-second Neminâtha, who were of the Harivaṃśa race.

All received *dîkshà* or consecration at their native places; and all obtained *jñâna* or complete enlightenment at the same, except Ṛishabha who became a *Kevalin* at Purimatàla, Nemi at Girnâr, and Mahâvîra at the Rijupàlukà river; and twenty of them died or obtained *moksha* (deliverance in bliss) on Sameta-Śikhara or Mount Pârśvanâtha in the west of Bengal. But Ṛishabha, the first, died on Ashṭâpada--supposed to be Śatruñljaya in Gujarât; Vâsupûjya died at Champâpuri in north Bengal; Neminâtha on mount Girnâr; and Mahâvîra, the last, at Pâvâpur.

Twenty-one of the Tîrthakaras are said to have attained Moksha in the Kâyotsarga (Guj. *Kâüsagga*) posture, and Ṛishabha, Nemi, and Mahâvira on the *padmâsana* or lotus throne.

For sake of brevity the following particulars for each Arhat are given below in serial order viz.:--

1. The *vimâna* or *vâhana* (heaven) from which he descended for incarnation.
2. Birthplace, and place of consecration or *dîkshâ*.
3. Names of father and mother.
4. Complexion.
5. Cognizance--*chihna* or *lâñchhaṇa*.
6. Height; and
7. Age.
8. Dîksha-vriksha or Bodhi tree.
9. Yaksha and Yakshiṇî, or attendant spirits.
10. First Ganadhara or leading disciple, and first Âryâ or leader of the female converts.

I. Ṛishabhadeva, Vṛishabha, Âdinthâ or Adiśvara Bhagavân:--(I) Sarvârthasiddha; (2) Vinittanagarî in Kośalâ and Purimatâla; (3) Nâbhîrâjâ by Marudevâ; (4) golden--*varṇa*-, (5)the bull,--*vṛisha, balada;* (6) 500 poles or *dhanusha*; (7) 8,400,000 pûrva or great years; (8) the Vaṭa or banyan tree; (9) Gomukha and Chakreśvarî; (10) Pundarîka and Brahmî.

II. Ajitanâtha: (1) Vijayavimàna; (2) Ayodhyâ; (3) Jitaśatru by Vijayâmâtâ; (4) golden; (5) the elephant--*gaja* or *hasti*; (6) 450 poles; (7)7,200,000 pûrva years; (8) Śâla--the Shorea robusta; (9) Mahâyaksha and Ajitabalâ: with the Digambaras, the Yakshiṇî is

Rohiṇî-yakshî; (10) Śiṁhasena and Phâlgu.

III. Sambhavanâtha: (1) Uvarîmagraiveka;(2) Sâvathi or Śràvasti; (3) Jitâri by Senâmâtâ; (4) golden; (5) the horse,--*aśva, ghoḍa*; (6) 400 poles; (7) 6,000,000 pûrva years; (8) the Prayâla--Buchanania latifolia; (9) Trimukha and Duritârî (Digambara--Prajñaptî); (10) Chàru and Śyâmâ.

IV. Abhinandana: (1) Jayantavimâna; (2) Ayodhyâ; (3) Sambararâjâ by Siddhârthà; (4) golden; (5) the ape,--*plavaga, vânara* or *kapi*; (6) 350 poles; (7) 5,000,000 pûrva years; (8) the Priyaṇgu or Panicum italicum; (9) Nàyaka and Kâlîkâ, and Digambara--Yaksheśvara and Vajraśṛiṅkhalâ; (10) Vajranâbha and Ajitâ.

V. Sumatinâtha: (1) Jayantavimâna; (2) Ayodhyâ; (3) Megharajâ by Maṅgalâ; (4) golden; (5) the curlew,--*krauṅcha*, (Dig. *chakravakapâkshâ*--the Brâhmani or red goose); (6) 300 poles; (7) 4,000,000 pûrva years; (8) Śâla tree; (9) Tuṁburu and Mahâkalî (Dig. Purushadattâ); (10) Charama and Kâśyapî.

VI. Padmaprabha: (1) Uvarîmagraiveka; (2) Kauśambî; (3) Śrîdhara by Susîmâ; (4) red (*rakta*); (5) a lotus bud--*padma, abja*, or *kamala*; (6) 250 poles; (7) 3,000,000 pûrva years; (8) the Chhatrâ --(Anethum sowa?); (9) Kusuma and Śyâmâ (Dig. Manovegâ or Manoguptî); (10) Pradyotana and Ratî.

VII. Supârśvanâtha: (1) Madhyamagraiveka; (2) Varâṇaśî; (3) Pratishṭharâjâ by Pṛithvî; (4) golden; [3] (5) the swastika symbol; (6) 200 poles; (7) 2,000,000 pûrva years; (8) the Śirîsha or Acacia sirisha; (9) Mâtaṅga and Śântâ;--Digambara, Varanandi and Kâlî; (10) Vidirbha and Somâ.

VIII. Chandraprabha: (1) Vijayanta; (2) Chandrapura; (3) Mahâsenarâjâ by Lakshmaṇâ; (4) white--*dhavala, śubhra*; (5) the moon--*chandrâ or śaśî*; (6) 150 poles; (7) 1,000,000 pûrva years; (8) the Nâga tree; (9) Vijaya and Bhṛikuṭî: Digambara--Śyâma or Vijaya and Jvâlâmâlinî; (10) Dinnâ and Sumanâ.

IX. Suvidhinâtha or Pushpadanta: (1) Ânatadevaloka; (2) Kânaṇḍînagarî; (3) Sugrîvarâja by Râmârâṇî; (4) white; (5) the

Makara (Dig. the crab--*êḍi*); (6) 100 poles; (7) 200,000 pûrva years; (8) the Śâlî; (9) Ajitâ and Sutârakâ: Digambara--Ajitâ and Mahâkâlî or Ajitâ; (10) Varâhaka and Vâruṇî.

X. Śitalanâtha: (1) Achyutadevaloka; (2)Bhadrapurâ or Bhadilapura; (3) Dṛiḍharatha-râjâ by Nandâ; (4) golden; (5) the Śrîvatsa figure: (Dig. *Śri-vriksha* the ficus religiosa); (6) 90 poles; (7) 100,000 pûrva years; (8) the Priyaṅgu tree; (9) Brahmâ and Aśokâ (Dig. Mânavî); (10) Nandâ and Sujasâ.

XI. Śreyâṁśanâtha or Śreyasa: (1) Achyutadevaloka; (2) Siṁhapurî; (3) Vishṇurâjâ by Vishṇâ; (4) golden; (5) the rhinoceros--*khaḍga, geṅḍâ*: (Dig. Garuḍa); (6) 80 poles; (7) 8,400,000 common years; (8) the Taṇḍuka tree; (9) Yaksheṭ and Mânavî: Digambara--Îśvara and Gauri; (10) Kaśyapa and Dhâraṇî.

XII. Vâsupûjya: (1) Prâṇatadevaloka; (2) Champâpurî; (3) Vasupûjya by Jayâ; (4) ruddy--*rakta*, Guj. *râtuṅ*; (5) the female buffalo--*mahishî, pâdâ*; (6) 70 poles; (7) 7,200,000 common years; (8) the Pâṭala or Bignonia suaveolens; (9) Kumâra and Chaṇḍâ (Dig. Gândhârî); (10) Subhuma and Dharaṇî.

XIII. Vimalanâtha: (1) Mahasâradevaloka; (2) Kampîlyapura; (3) Kṛitavarmarâja by Śyâmâ; (4) golden; (5) a boar--*śâkara, varâha*; (6) 60 poles; (7) 6,000,000 years; (8) the Jâmbu or Eugenia jambolana; (9) Shâṇmukha and Viditâ (Dig. Vairôṭî); (10) Mandara and Dharâ.

XIV. Anantanâtha or Anantajit: (1) Prâṇatadevaloka; (2) Ayodhyâ; (3) Siṁhasena by Suyaśâh[postvocalic] or Sujasâ; (4) golden; (5) a falcon--*śyena* (Dig. *bhallûka* a bear); (6) 50 poles; (7) 3,000,000 years; (8) the Aśoka or Jonesia asoka; (9) Pâtâla and Ankuśâ (Dig. Anantamatî); (10) Jasa and Padmâ.

XV. Dharmanâtha: (1) Vijayavimâna; (2) Ratnapurî; (3) Bhânurâjâ by Suvritâ; (4) golden; (5) the thunderbolt--*vajra*; (6) 45 poles; (7) 1,000,000 years; (8) Dadhîparṇa tree (Clitoria ternatea?); (9) Kinnara and Kandarpâ (Dig. Mânasî); (10) Arishṭa and Ârthaśivâ.

XVI. Śântinâthâ: (1) Sarvârthasiddha; (2) Gajapura or Hastinapurî;

(3) Viśvasena by Achirâ; (4) golden; (5) an antelope--*mṛiga, haraṇa, hullĕ,* (6)40 poles; (7) 100,000 years; (8) the Nandî or Cedrela toona; (9) Garuḍa and Nirvâṇî (Dig. Kimpurusha and Mahâmânasî); (10) Chakrâyuddha and Suchî.

XVII. Kunthtinâtha: (1) Sarvârthasiddha; (2) Gajapura; (3) Sûrarâjâ by Śrîrânî; (4) golden; (5) a goat--*chhâga* or *aja*; (6) 35 poles; (7) 95,000 years; (8) the Bhilaka tree; (9) Gandharva and Balâ (Dig. Vijayâ); (10) Sâmba and Dâminî.

XVIII. Aranâtha: (1) Sarvârthasiddha; (2) Gajapura; (3) Sudarśana by Devîrâṇî; (4) golden; (5) the Nandyâvarta diagram, (Dig. *Mina*--the zodiacal Pisces); (6) 30 poles; (7) 84,000 years; (8) Âmbâ or Mango tree; (9) Yaksheṭa and Dhaṇâ (Dig. Kendra and Ajitâ); (10) Kumbha and Rakshitâ.

XIX. Mallinâtha: (1) Jayantadevaloka; (2) Mathurâ; (3) Kumbharâjâ by Prabhâvatî; (4) blue--*nîla*; (5) a jar--*kumbham, kalaśa* or *ghaṭa*; (6) 25 poles; (7) 55,000 years; (8) Aśoka tree; (9) Kubera and Dharaṇapriyâ (Dig. Aparâjitâ); (10) Abhikshaka and Bandhumatî.

XX. Munisuvrata, Suvrata or Muni: (1) Aparâjita-devaloka; (2) Râjagṛiha; (3) Sumitrarâjâ by Padmâvatî; (4) black--*śyâma, asita*; (5) a tortoise--*kûrma*; (6) 20 poles; (7) 30,000 years; (8) the Champaka, Michelia champaka; (9) Varuṇa and Naradattâ, (Dig. Bahurûpiṇî); (10) Malli and Pushpavatî.

XXI. Naminâtha, Nimi or Nimeśvara: (1) Prâṇatadevaloka; (2) Mathurâ; (3) Vijayarâjâ by Viprârâṇî; (4) yellow; (5) the blue water-lily--*nîlotpala*, with the Digambaras, sometimes the Aśoka tree; (6) 15 poles; (7) 10,000 years; (8) the Bakula or Mimusops elengi; (9) Bhṛikuṭi and Gandhârî, (Dig. Châmuṇḍî); (10) Śubha and Anilâ.

XXII. Neminâtha or Arishṭanemi: (1) Aparâjita; (2) Sauripura (Prákrit--Soriyapura) and Ujjinta or Mount Girnâr; (3) Samudravijaya by Śivâdevi; (4) black--*śyâma*; (5) a conch,--*śaṅkha*; (6) 10 poles; (7) 1000 years; (8) the Veṭasa; (9) Gomedha and Ambikâ: with the Digambaras, Sarvâhṇa and Kûshmâṇḍinî; (10) Varadatta and Yakshadinnâ.

XXIII. Pârśvanâtha: (1) Prâṇatadevaloka; (2) Varâṇasî and Sameta-Śikhara; (3) Aśvasenarâja by Vâmâdevî; (4) blue--*nîla*; (5) a serpent--*sarpa*; (6) 9 hands; (7) 100 years; (8) the Dhâtakî or Grislea tomentosa; (9) Pârśvayaksha or Dharaṇendra and Padmâvatî; (10) Âryadinna and Pushpachûḍâ.

XXIV. Śri-Mahâvîra, Vardhamâna or Vîra, the Śramaṇa: (1) Prâṇ atadevaloka; (2) Kuṇḍagrâma or Chitrakûṭa, and Ṛijupâlukâ; (3) Siddhârtharâja, Śreyânśa or Yaśasvin by Triśalâ Vidchadinnâ or Priyakâriṇî; (4) yellow; (5) a lion--*keśarî-simha*; (6) 7 hands or cubits; (7) 72 years; (8) the *śala* or teak tree; (9) Mâtaṁga and Siddhâyikâ; (10) Indrabhûti and Chandrabâlâ.

The Tirthakuras may be regarded as the *dii majores* of the Jainas, [4] though, having become Siddhas, emancipated from all concern, they can have no interest in mundane affairs. They and such beings as are supposed to have reached perfection are divided into fifteen species:

1. Tîrthakarasiddhas;
2. Atîrthakarasiddhas;
3. Tîrthasiddhas;
4. Svaliṅgasiddas;
5. Anyaliṅgasiddhas;
6. Striliṅgasiddhas;
7. Purushaliṅgasiddhas;
8. Napuṁsakaliṅgasiddhas;
9. Gṛihaliṅgasiddhas;
10. Tîrthavyavachchhedasiddhas;
11. Pratyekabuddhasiddhas;
12. Svayambuddhasiddhas;
13. Ekasiddas;
14. Anekasiddhas;
15. Buddhabodhietasiddllas.

[5]

But the gods are divided into four classes, and each class into several orders: the four classes are:--

I. Bhavanâdhipatis, Bhavanavâsins or Bhaumeyikas, of

which there are ten orders, viz.--

1. Asurakumâras;
2. Nâgakumâras;
3. Taḍitkumâras or Vidyutkumâras;
4. Suvarṇa- or Suparnaka-kumâras;
5. Agnikumâras;
6. Dvîpakumâras (Dîvakumâras);
7. Udadhikumâras;
8. Dikkumâras;
9. Pavana- or Vâta-kumâras;
10. Ghaṇika- or Sanitakumâras.

II. Vyantaras or Vâṇamantaras, who live in woods are of eight classes:--

1. Piśâchas;
2. Bhûtas;
3. Yakshas;
4. Râkshasas;
5. Kimnaras;
6. Kimpurushas;
7. Mahoragas;
8. Gandharvas.

III. The Jyotishkas are the inhabitants of;

1. Chandras or the moons;
2. Sûryas or the suns;
3. Grahas or the planets;
4. Nakshatras or the constellations;
5. Târâs or the hosts of stars.

And IV. The Vaimânika gods are of two orders: (1) the Kalpabhavas, who are born in the heavenly Kalpas; and (2) the Kalpâtîtas, born in the regions above the Kalpas.

(1) The Kalpabhavas again are subdivided into twelve genera who live in the Kalpas after which they are named; viz,--

1. Saudharma;
2. Îśâna;
3. Sanatkumâra;
4. Mâhendra;
5. Brahmaloka;
6. Lântaka;

7. Śukra or Mahâśukla;
8. Sahasrâra;
9. Ânata (Âṇaya);
10. Prâṇata (Pâṇaya);
11. Âraṇa;
12. Achyuta.

(2) The Kalpâtîtas are subdivided into-- (a) the Graiveyakas, living on the upper part of the universe; and (b) the Anuttaras or those above whom there are no others.

(a) The Graiveyakas are of nine species, viz.--

1. Sudarsaṇas;
2. Supratipandhas;
3. Maṇoramas;
4. Sarvabhadras;
5. Suviśâlas;
6. Somaṇasas;
7. Sumaṅkasas;
8. Prîyaṅkaras;
9. Âdityas or Nandikaras.

(b) the Anuttara gods are of five orders: viz.--

1. Vijayas;
2. Vaijayantas;
3. Jayantas;
4. Aparâjitas; and
5. Sarvârthasiddhas.

[6]

These Anuttara gods inhabit the highest heavens where they live for varying lengths of time as the heavens ascend; and in the fifth or highest--the great Vimâna called Sarvârthasiddha--they all live thirty-three Sâgaropamas or periods of unimagiable duration. Still all the gods are mortal or belong to the *saṁsâra*.

Above these is the paradise of the Siddhas or perfected souls, and the *Uttarâdhyana Sûtra* gives the following details of this realm of the perfected, or the paradise of the Jainas:-- [7]

"The perfected souls are those of women, men, hermaphrodites, of orthodox, heterodox, and householders. Perfection is reached by people of the greatest, smallest and middle size; [8] on high places, underground, on the surface of the earth, in the ocean, and in waters (of rivers, etc.).

"Ten hermaphrodites reach perfection at the same time, twenty women, one hundred and eight men; four householders, ten heterodox, and one hundred and eight orthodox monks.

"Two individuals of the greatest size reach perfection (simultaneously), four of the smallest size, and one hundred and eight of the middle size. Four individuals reach perfection (simultaneously) on high places, two in the ocean, three in water, twenty underground; and where do they go on reaching perfection? Perfected souls are debarred from the non-world (Aloka); they reside on the top of the world; they leave their bodies here (below) and go there, on reaching perfection.

"Twelve *yojanas* above the (Vimâna) Sarvârtha is the place called Îshatpragbhâra, which has the form of an umbrella; (there the perfected souls go). It is forty-five hundred thousand *yojanas* long, and as many broad, and it is somewhat more than three times as many in circumference. Its thickness is eight *yojanas*, it is greatest in the middle, and decreases towards the margin, till it is thinner than the wing of a fly. This place, by nature pure, consisting of white gold, resembles in form an open umbrella, as has been said by the best of Jinas.

"(Above it) is a pure blessed place (called Śîtâ), which is white like a conch-shell, the *anka*-stone, and Kunda-flowers; [9] a *yojana* thence is the end of the world. The perfected souls penetrate the sixth part of the uppermost *krośa* of the (above-mentioned) *yojana*. There, at the top of the world reside the blessed perfected souls, rid of all transmigration, and arrived at the excellent state of perfection. The dimension of a perfected soul is two-thirds of the height which the individual had in his last existence.

"The perfected souls considered singly--*êgattêṇa* (as individuals)--have a beginning but no end, considered collectively--*puhuttêṇa* (as a class)--they have neither a beginning nor an end. They have no (visible) form, they consist of life throughout, they are developed into knowledge and faith, they have crossed the boundary of the Saṁsâra, and reached the excellent state of perfection."

Like both the Brâhmaṇs and Buddhists, the Jainas have a series of hells--Nârakas, numbering even which they name--

1. Ratnaprabhâ;
2. Śarkarâprabhâ;
3. Vâlukâprabhâ;
4. Paṅkaprabhâ;
5. Dhûmaprabhâ;
6. Tamaprabhâ;
7. Tamatamaprabhâ.

[10]

Those who inhabit the seventh hell have a stature of 500 poles, and in each above that they are half the height of the one below it.

Everything in the system as to stature of gods and living beings, their ages and periods of transmigration is reduced to artificial numbers.

The Jaina Gachhas.

About the middle of the tenth century there flourished a Jaina high priest named Uddyotana, with whose pupils the eighty four gachhas originated. This number is still spoken of by the Jainas, but the lists that have been hitherto published are very discordant. The following was obtained from a member of the sect as being their recognised list,-- and allowing for differences of spelling, nearly every name may be recognised in those previously published by Mr. H. G. Briggs or Colonel Miles.

The Eighty four Gachchhas of the Jainas. [11]

1. ? *†
2. Osvâla*†
3. Âṅchala*
4. Jirâvalâ*†
5. Khaḍatara or Kharatara
6. Lonkâ or Richmati*†
7. Tapâ*†
8. Gaṁgeśvara*†
9. Koraṇṭavâla†
10. Ânandapura†
11. Bharavalî
12. Uḍhavîyâ*†
13. Gudâvâ*†
14. Dekâüpâ or Dekâwâ*†
15. Bh nmâlâ†
16. Mahuḍîyâ*†
17. Gachhapâla*†
18. Goshavâla†
19. Magatragagadâ†
20.
22. Vîkaḍîyâ*†
23. Muñjhîyâ*†
24. Chitroḍâ†
25. Sâchorâ*†
26. Jachaṇḍîyâ†
27. Sîdhâlavâ*†
28. Mîyâṇṇîyâ
29. Âgamîyâ†
30. Maladhârî*†
31. Bhâvarîyâ†
32. Palîvâla*†
33. Nâgadîgeśvara†
34. Dharmaghosha†
35. Nâgapurâ*†
36. Uchatavâla†
37. Nâṇṇâvâla*†
38. Sâḍerâ*†
39. Maṇḍovarâ*†
40. Śurâṇî*†
41. Khaṁbhâvatî*†
43. Sopârîyâ*†
44. Mâṇḍalîyâ*†
45. Kochhîpanâ*†
46. Jâgaṁna*†
47. Lâparavâla*†
48. Vosaraḍâ*†
49. Düîvaṅdanîyâ*†
50. Chitrâvâla*†
51. Vegaḍâ
52. Vâpaḍâ
53. Vîjaharâ, Vîjharâ*†
54. Kâüpurî†
55. Kâchala
56. Haṁdalîyâ†
57. Mahukarâ†
58. Putaliyâ*†
59. Kaṁnarîsey†
60. Revarḍîyâ*†
61. Dhandhukâ†
62. Thaṁbhanîpaṇâ*
63. Paṁchîvâla†
64. Pâlaṇ
65. Gaṁdhâr
66. Velîyâ
67. Sâḍhapur
68. Nagarakc
69. Hâsoı
70. Bhaṭanerâ
71. Jaṇah
72. Jagây
73. Bhîmaser
74. Takaç
75. Kaṁt
76. Senat
77. Vaghe
78. Vaheç
79. Siddhapu
80. Ghog
81. Nîgaı
82. Punaı
83. Varha

Vṛihmânîyâ† | 84. Nâmî
21. Tâlârâ*†

Sketch of Jaina Mythology

FOOTNOTES

Footnote 1: See *Ratnasâgara*, bh. II, pp. 696--705.
Footnote 2: *Cave Temples*, pp. 491, 496; *Arch. Sur. Westn. India*, vol. I, p. 25 and pl. xxxvii; vol. V, p. 49; *Transactions, R. As. Soc.*, vol. I, p. 435. At Rânpur in Godwâr, in the temple of Rishabhanâtha is a finely carved slab representing Pârśvanâtha in the Kâyotsarga position, attended by snake divinities,--*Archit. and Scenery in Gujarât and Râjputâna*, p. 21. The story has variants: conf. *Ind. Ant.* vol. XXX, p. 302.
Footnote 3: The Digambara describe the colours of the seventh and twenty-first Jinas as *marakada* or emerald coloured.
Footnote 4: For an account of the ritual of the Svetâmbara sect of Jainas, see my account in the *Indian Antiquary*, vol. XIII, pp. 191-196.
Footnote 5: *Jour. Asiat.* IXme Ser. tom. XIX, p. 260.
Footnote 6: Conf. *Ratnasâgara*, bh. II, pp. 616, 617; *Jour. Asiat.* IXme Ser. tome XIX, p. 259; *Sac. Bks. E.* vol. XLV, p. 226 f. See also *Rev. de l'Histoire des Relig.* tom. XLVII, pp. 34-50, which has appeared since the above was written, for "La doctrine des êtres vivants dans la Religion Jaina".
Footnote 7: See *ante*, p. 11, note 10; The following extract is from *Sac. Books of the East*, vol. XLV, pp. 211-213.
Footnote 8: The greatest size--*ogâhaṇâ*--of men is

Footnote 8: The greatest size--*ogâhaṇâ*--of men is 500 dhanush or 2000 cubits, the smallest is one cubit.

Footnote 9: The gourd Lagenaria vulgaris.

Footnote 10: *Ratnasâgara*, bh. II, p. 607; *Jour. As.* u.s. p. 263.

Footnote 11: Those names marked * are found in Col. Miles's list *Tr. R. A. S.* vol. III, pp. 358 f. 363, 365, 370. Those marked † are included in H. G. Brigg's list,--*Cities of Gujarashtra*, p. 339.

www.ingramcontent.com/pod-product-compliance
Lightning Source LLC
Chambersburg PA
CBHW020110170426
43199CB00009B/479